Praise for The Microsoft Teams Playbook

"The Microsoft Teams Playbook is just that: a book that empowers teachers to be their own classroom coaches while also giving them practical Microsoft tools to empower the learning of their students. I really enjoy the sports analogies and practical advice sprinkled throughout the book and the Time Outs built throughout to add points of reflection. Throughout the book I can feel the support of Jenallee like a coach encouraging me to improve my teaching game. I'm fired up!"

—**Carl Hooker,** educational consultant and strategist

"Jeni Long and Salleé Clark have created a robust resource for educators! If you are a Microsoft Teams user, this is a must-read, full of ideas and inspiration you can bring into your classroom right away. This book would be a great choice for a book club or PLC focused on creating equitable learning experiences for students.

"If you are committed to making your classroom accessible for all students, *The Microsoft Teams Playbook* provides practical, actionable advice to make an impact throughout the school year."

—**Monica Burns,** EdD, author of *EdTech Essentials: The Top 10 Technology Strategies for All Learning Environments*

"Maybe you are still learning to navigate a digital classroom and don't know where to start. No worries!" (Ch. 5) Jeni and Salleé bring together their experience and expertise to offer this practical guide for today's educator. From building relationships to cultivating equitable classrooms to using top tech tools to engage and empower students, the dynamic duo of Jenallee has us covered! *The Microsoft Teams Playbook* leaves me feeling excited for the future and eager to see what readers create with their students!"

—**Dr. Jennifer Williams,** executive director, Take Action Global, author of *Teach Boldly: Using Edtech for Social Good*

"Jeni and Salleé have written a modern Teams playbook and share top tips and strategies to help you empower teaching and learning in new ways! Throughout *The Microsoft Teams Playbook*, you will gain insights and ideas that help level up your skills with tools like Microsoft Teams, Whiteboard, PowerPoint, Flipgrid, and more. This dynamic duo, aka #Jenallee, not only delivers an inspiring message to help get you mentally prepared, but they also deliver a whole bunch of awesome play-by-play directions and coach you with best practices to make learning more inclusive, interactive, accessible and engaging for all. Tighten your laces and jump right in. You'll be glad you did!"

—**Ann Kozma,** educator innovation lead, Flipgrid

"Jeni and Salleé's, *The Microsoft Teams Playbook*, shares a personal journey into how educators can facilitate an equitable classroom for students. Step-by-step, they teach you how to develop stronger student relationships that can help drive your instruction to meet their interests. With this book, the power is in your hands!"

—Joe and Kristin Merrill, first and fourth grade teachers, coauthors of *the InterACTIVE Class* Series

"Jeni and Salleé have created a coaching manual for you and your classroom and have included practical tips, personal stories, and time for you to reflect and evaluate what you're reading. They include an entire chapter on accessibility, share lesson ideas and how-tos for utilizing educational technology tools you're probably already using! Even if you're not a Microsoft user, *The Microsoft Teams Playbook* is structured in a way that any teacher can pick it up and immediately implement it to better engage their students!"

—Tisha Poncio, digital learning specialist

"*The Microsoft Teams Playbook* is a must read for teachers, coaches, and anyone in education! Jeni and Salleé share their heart, creativity, and passion through their practical ideas. Their book spans across a wonderful variety of equally important Teams topics like building relationships, feedback, setting expectations, and more. Whether you're teaching remotely, hybrid, or in person, you'll find great value in not only reading this book once but referring to it time after time!"

—Scott Titmas, community engagement manager, Flipgrid

"If it's Jenallee, it's golden! In *The Microsoft Teams Playbook*, Jenallee has put their heart into supporting and empowering educators who in turn empower all students! Both Jeni and Salleé are passionate educators and also moms who truly live what they are sharing in The Microsoft Teams Playbook. Readers will feel like they personally know Jeni and Salleé and will get the true coaching support and encouragement one would be inspired by. Jenallee coaches readers through tools, ideas, and pedagogy to leverage the digital classrooms we are in. Giving "Time Out" moments for reflection make this a must read for any educator looking to begin using or level up their Microsoft Teams usage in the classroom!"

—Andy Knueven, digital learning coach and professional learning specialist

"Unlike professionals who work in the private sector, teachers spend most of the day with children in classrooms. I fully understand they are teaching, and their job is to be in front of students; however, we should be working tirelessly to find new ways for educators to work together, and this book is like a collaboration with two amazing educational leaders.

"Jeni and Salleé's book, *The Microsoft Teams Playbook*, uses words and ideas to open the metaphorical door to classrooms and a world of dynamic learning. The Microsoft Teams Playbook gives an inside look and robust ideas to empower and encourage educators to maximize learning anywhere and anytime."

—Dr. Matthew X. Joseph, district leader

"*The Microsoft Teams Playbook* is the book I've been needing to finally bring the power of Microsoft teams into the multilayered needs of my classroom. Jeni and Salleé have created the go-to guide to coach me through the process as I synthesize tools and pedagogy for engaging and impactful learning for all students."

—**Lisa Highfill,** coauthor of *The HyperDoc Handbook* and
co-creator of Teachers Give Teachers

"We recently had the good fortune of reading this book, and we both agreed it is a book that should be a must for educators and coaches. It is a well-written book, easy and fun to read, and full of resources and tips to improve your practice. Thank you Jeni and Salleé for helping educators around the world."

—**Alberto & Mario Herraez,** The eTwinz, international speakers and global teachers

"Teaching in today's technology-enhanced schools is like being the underdog in the championship game. But don't worry, with this book you've got two great coaches—Jeni and Salleé—who will empower you with a game plan that includes accessible, equitable, and relationship-focused pedagogical practices. With the dozens of edtech examples and lesson ideas in this book, my money is on you hoisting that championship trophy!"

—**Jake Miller,** teacher, author, podcaster, speaker

"Like that song by Snap, 'The Power,' Jenallee snaps ya awake and riles you up! In an instant, you are pumped and empowered to do amazing things. Having seen these two share, I am proud to endorse their great work. There is really something for everyone from the new teacher to the veteran that knows all the tricks of the trade. I can attest to their love of helping people and genuinely setting out to help them where they are.

"This book has classroom strategies, advice, pro tips, and has a plethora of tech goodness, but most of all it prioritizes people—our greatest resource and our greatest joy in education. Their stories will move you, and I second their position on the power of the PLN! I would not be the educator I am without my network and MIE Community. I am blessed to know them, learn from them, and have been to dozens of conferences and professional development opportunities, and I can attest that they know how to truly empower in a lasting way."

—**Scott Nunes,** educational technology coach, podcaster, speaker

The Microsoft TEAMS Playbook

Your Guide to Creating an Empowered Classroom

Tips, Plans, and Strategies for Fostering Accessible and Equitable Learning Environments

Jeni Long & Sallee Clark

#Jenallee

The Microsoft Teams Playbook
© 2021 by Jeni Long and Salleé Clark

These books are available at special discounts when purchased in quantity for use as premiums, promotions, fundraising, and educational use. For inquiries and details, contact the publisher: elevatebooksedu.com

Published by Elevate Books EDU

Editing and Interior Design by My Writers' Connection
Cover design by Genesis Kohler

Library of Congress Control Number: 2021948970
Paperback ISBN: 978-1-7352046-9-7

eBook ISBN: 979-8-9851374-0-8

DEDICATION

To our families—
Thank you for supporting our long nights of collaboration, brainstorming,
and writing. Your support in reaching our goals means the world to us.

To our mentors—
Thank you for sharing your wisdom and guiding us as we
embark on this new writing journey.

To our PLN and the entire MIE Expert family—
Thank you for your friendship, collaboration, and kindness.
We love learning with you and sharing edtech goodness
with this amazing community of educators.

To our work family, the teachers, and students at
Eagle Mountain-Saginaw ISD—
Thank you for inspiring us daily. We appreciate your encouragement,
collaboration, and support as we use edtech solutions shared in this book.

Contents

FOREWORD

Jeni Long and Salleé Clark's work first came to my attention when the Microsoft Education product team that I work on learned about the amazing things happening at the Eagle Mountain-Saginaw School District in Texas. This was in the early days of the OneNote Class Notebook. I hopped on a call to learn more about the school district, and that's where I met Jeni and Salleé. I learned how they had not only helped roll out OneNote EDU across their district but also had helped train, coach, innovate, and inspire educators in their district to effectively use this tool in the classroom.

I became intrigued with this dynamic duo (a.k.a. #Jenallee) and started talking with them more, collaborating, co-presenting, and learning with them. We've had so much fun, and I really value the friendship that we've developed. I've been able to watch them continue to inspire, innovate, and coach educators during the past few years. The three of us have even started experimenting with new professional development formats on TikTok. I'm so glad that they are able to share their wisdom with you.

Jeni and Salleé have put together a book that wraps many of my favorite edtech topics into a highly effective package. Using their extensive background in both education and tech coaching, they've embedded practical and applicable strategies in this playbook that will help all educators.

Whether your school is doing in person classes or using a hybrid or remote model—or something in-between—*The Microsoft Teams Playbook* will help you prepare, implement, and get the most out of your edtech tools to improve learning outcomes.

The structure of the book works perfectly. I love how they've used the coaching metaphor throughout to break down the different aspects, from the rules of the game to best practices, coaching, scouting, and running plays. Jeni and Salleé have also meticulously curated real-world examples, tips, tools, and templates you can easily bring into your classroom via QR codes and links. You might say this book covers all the bases and is a grand slam!

Jeni and Salleé have built a thorough set of expertise across not only Microsoft products in education, but many of the innovative edtech products that integrate with Teams. They cover many of the products that I personally work on, such as Microsoft Teams, OneNote and our Accessibility tools. As someone who helps build many of these products, I can firmly say that

Jeni and Salleé have an expert grasp on the details, as well as the educator and coaching skills to match. They have also built relationships with Microsoft team members, given us early product feedback, co-presented with us, and deeply understand the scenarios for the classroom. This includes all forms of education that have happened before and after March 2020, when much of the United States went to some form of remote learning.

Outside of Microsoft products, they are ambassadors for so many other great education tools. Jeni and Salleé even made introductions between partners like Whiteboard.chat and me, which helped us collaborate to add Immersive Reader to Whiteboard.chat and a new Teams integration. So, as you can see, #Jenallee offers the full package and their expertise shines through in *The Microsoft Teams Playbook.*

I encourage you to make the most of the valuable lessons, examples, and tips in this book. Share it with other educators and your school's leaders. Don't be afraid to take chances and try new things. You have two of the best coaches around to help you on your journey!

—**Mike Tholfsen**
Principal Group Product Manager, Microsoft Education

PREFACE

Hello! We are Jeni Long and Salleé Clark. Together we are "Jenallee" (more about this in a bit) and bring nearly 40 years of collective educational experience as teachers, librarians, and technology specialists. Currently, we are instructional technologists with Eagle Mountain-Saginaw Independent School District in Fort Worth, Texas—the best job in the world. We coach teachers to infuse their lessons with technology. Seeing them empower their students with critical thinking skills and empathy makes us proud to know technology is bringing real life into their classrooms.

We are passionate and dedicated educators, but we are moms first—moms of amazing children who helped us recognize students learn in different ways. Our kiddos inspired this book. They influenced our vision of what the classroom should look like and motivated us to help other teachers create equitable and accessible classrooms for their students. Say hello to Payton Long and Hunter Clark.

Payton Long

Payton, the oldest of my (Jeni's) four children, is motivated, driven, organized, and determined. She is a leader and a bit bossy. (I admit she comes by the bossy naturally.) But Payton struggled at an early age to properly identify letters and numbers and, even though I was trained as an educator to identify the needs of students, I didn't notice her difficulty.

When Payton was in second grade, my mother, a special education expert, recognized early signs that Payton might have dyslexia. My mom worked with her on a regular basis to identify numbers on playing cards and, fortunately, recognized Payton needed to have some testing done to determine whether she was dyslexic. The summer before her third-grade year, Payton was diagnosed with dyslexia and, fortunately, received services during the third grade and made tremendous gains.

The following year we moved to Tennessee and, because dyslexia was not recognized as a disability, Payton did not receive services. I had to work very closely with her teachers each year to put supports in place to assure Payton's success. We determined Payton excelled with oral accommodations and use of colored overlays. She especially liked using a tracker to keep the words from bouncing all over the page when she read. We worked as a team to ensure Payton had what she needed to be successful. She also learned to advocate for herself and to overcome her challenges by finding the tools to help relieve her stress. But it was not easy. We spent many nights crying and talking about her pains and joys. As a mom, I suffer when my children suffer, but I also celebrate when they celebrate! Payton is now a senior and has a lot to celebrate. I think her own words express best her success:

> In elementary school, I felt different from the other students. Math and reading were extremely hard for me, and I believed they would always be difficult. I still struggle with my dyslexia and comprehension, but I continue to persevere to become a stronger student. Even with my dyslexia, I can maintain the A/B honor roll every year even while taking higher-level classes. Over the years of pushing myself beyond my limits, I have learned how to deal with dyslexia. I do not like to call it a "learning disability" because I can learn just as well as the smartest kid in class. I might need more time or extra help, but that does not make me any less smart. I have learned to embrace my differences and help others who struggle like I have.

Payton's experiences from the eighth grade forward validate my purpose for writing this book. When she moved into the Eagle Mountain-Saginaw Independent School District, she received the help and support she needed to succeed. Every teacher understood her struggles and treated her the same as the other kids. This helped her push herself, break past her barriers, and learn more about herself.

Payton is an overcomer. Your job as educators is to empower children like Payton with the necessary tools and skills to embrace their differences and help them overcome their struggles.

Hunter Clark

Hunter is my (Salleé's) brave and creative son. He is a strategic gamer, tech guru, and rock enthusiast. This awesome kid has been an overcomer from day one. He was born with clubfoot; both of Hunter's feet were turned inward. Medical professionals are unclear as to why this happens to one in one thousand babies, but without medical attention, Hunter eventually would have walked on the tops of his feet.

At Scottish Rite Hospital, Hunter was placed in casts when he was four days old, and we continued casting for five weeks. Hunter then wore corrective shoes for the first year of his life and underwent his first surgery when he was in kindergarten. The surgeons broke both of his tibias to turn them and aligned them correctly with plates. Hunter was in a wheelchair with double leg casts for six weeks. A year later, Hunter returned to Scottish Rite for a second surgery to remove the plates.

Medical professionals really do make miracles happen. Today you would have no idea Hunter was born with clubfoot; he walks like you and me. It is beautiful!

But Hunter is so much more than clubfoot. He displays his curiosity, ingenious observations, outside-the-box thinking, and empathy every day. This young scholar also has an amazing memory. As an elementary student, he could listen to and read a guided reading book one time, and it was committed to memory. His teachers ran out of guided reading books for him!

As we continued to enjoy reading and learning at home, I noticed he could spell words like cat and dog; however, when I showed him the word to read, he had no idea what the word was. I knew his memory was good, but I was fairly certain he was not reading phonetically. My mom was instrumental in helping me determine that Hunter had dyslexia. As a principal and former special education teacher, she joined me in my efforts to evaluate Hunter's reading progress. She encouraged us to look into testing Hunter for dyslexia. We returned to Scottish Rite for testing, and Hunter was diagnosed with dyslexia and attention deficit hyperactivity disorder (ADHD).

This intelligent young man did not fit the mold of school. He enjoyed creating over writing, and he enjoyed exploring the world instead of looking at it through a book. Hunter's insights helped me understand his struggle and made me a better advocate for him. Here's what Hunter says:

> Dyslexia makes learning hard. Words move on the page, making it very difficult to read and understand what I am reading. I have to work hard to learn, but tools like Immersive Reader, line focus, dictation, and audio books help make learning a little easier. Dyslexia isn't all bad; there are some good things about dyslexia. I have a good imagination, I think outside of the box, and dyslexia makes me different from others and that is a good thing. I am smart and I know that my strengths will help me now and in the future.

This journey has not been easy, but it has been rich with perseverance. And I have realized, through advocating for Hunter so he had access to learning, I am really advocating to empower every child in the classroom with the tools they need to learn.

Scan this QR code to read an article highlighting Payton and Hunter as they share their journey of how using Immersive Reader has impacted their learning journey.

From Challenge to Superpower

Hunter and Payton do not fit into the box of "traditional education," where many educators wanted them to live. We are not alone in this thought. In his Microsoft Educator Center (MEC) course, Made by Dyslexia, Josh Clark says, "Dyslexic child(ren) are not made for the traditional classroom; they are made for the world. And it's because they see things differently." Josh is right. People with dyslexia—and other learning challenges—process information differently, which means they have unique insight into situations and problems. So, their challenges are actually superpowers!

We do not want students to have to fit into the mold of school; we want school to fit their individual needs. In spite of multiple challenges, 2020 gave us a glimpse into how teaching differently can potentially meet different needs. Our hope is for all students to love learning and have the same opportunity to learn. We want all students to be on the same playing field as their peers and, ultimately, find their passions and pursue them with excitement.

This book is our attempt to help you recognize the diversity of student learning needs in your classroom, understand the need for differentiated instruction, and use technology to create a more equitable and accessible classroom. Dyslexia and ADHD are just two challenges to learning that can be overcome with differentiated instruction. Every classroom includes unique personalities, struggles, successes, and needs. Every student in your classroom has a unique story and needs an advocate—someone who will meet them where they are and get to know them and what they need to learn. *This* is education. *This* is what *all* students deserve.

Our children significantly influenced our views, suggestions, and thoughts. We watched them struggle, fail, and succeed, and we learned how to support them in the process. Our experiences as moms of children with dyslexia give us a unique perspective. As tech coaches and educators, we know how important it is for *all* students to be on the same playing field; we want *all* students to have equal access to content, tools, student agency, and opportunities. Our goal is for this book to equip you to offer those things to every student in your classroom and give them hope that they will receive an equitable, genuine, and relevant education. We are writing this book to empower you to foster a blended learning environment that is accessible and equitable for all! We want to give you *POWER*:

P • develop purposeful lessons that make learning accessible and relevant to all learners

purpose

O • offer your students opportunities to build student agency, set learning goals, and to take risks in their learning

Opportunity

W • ask you to stretch your views, evaluate yourself, and be willing to change your teaching so that all students have the opportunity to learn

willing

E • offer you resources and ideas for implementing lessons through Microsoft Teams that engage all learners

engage

R 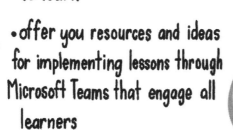 • see the need and importance to put your students first... to create an equal playing field within your classroom

Relationships

@woodard_julie

A New Teaching Day Dawns

Classroom 1

Hello, online learners! Hello…? Are you there? I only see circles with your initials. If you want, you can turn on your cameras—I would love to see your smiling faces. [cameras come on] *Oh, yay! Hello, Audrey! Pancakes for breakfast? Delicious! Hello, James. Nice Power Ranger pj's!* [James gives a "demonstration"] *Yes, James, you do have moves like the Red Ranger. Impressive!*

Classroom 2

Hi, Dan, welcome to the classroom! ["Air" high five, temperature check, hand sanitizer squirt] *Good morning, Olivia! So glad you're here!* ["Air" fist bump, "right foot left foot bump," temperature check, hand sanitizer squirt] *Hello, Alexis! Welcome to class!* ["Air" hug, "eye" smile, temperature check, hand sanitizer squirt] *As you come into the classroom, get started on your bell work at your desk.*

Classroom 3

Kidz Bop music on? Check. Breakfast cart stocked? Check. Bell work on the table? Check. Kids online ready? Check.

Welcome to class, friends! One squirt of hand sanitizer and grab a breakfast sack. Enjoy these awesome tunes as you eat breakfast. When you finish you can begin the bell work.

My friends online, I hope your breakfast is delicious! When you finish, make sure you are ready for the day, teeth brushed, clothes on, and then head to your at-home workstation and join us for bell work.

Does this sound familiar?

In March of 2020, education as we knew it abruptly stopped. With the rise of Covid-19 cases in the United States, schools across the country closed their doors and opened remote classrooms. Almost overnight, all teachers became "first-year teachers" again as they learned how to teach their students online. During the early days of the pandemic, teaching got flipped on its head, spun around, and shaken, ten times over.

Whether your morning routine was like the scenario above or a variation of it, you are a teacher who taught during 2020. We applaud *you*! You juggled online lessons and in-person learning activities, you struggled with "mask rash," called your online students after school to conduct one-on-one tutoring sessions—and *so many more* tasks that were not part of your pre-Covid responsibilities. Your hard work and dedication to student learning is evident, and we are in awe of *you*! We applaud you, personally, and everything you do as a teacher.

Thankfully, like you, we survived those dizzying days. Even though we are still catching our breath a bit, during this time of blended, in-person, and online learning, we discovered some new tools that not only helped us teach remotely, but also made our classrooms more equitable and accessible for our students—something we are passionate about.

Through the Covid pandemic, we saw our teachers step up to the plate with inventive lessons, reaching far beyond paper, pencil, computers, and online tools. We are in awe of everything they did in these various learning environments and so thankful we got to coach them through this hard time of learning. This experience opened our eyes to the importance of empowering teachers and students.

Coach's Manual

Individually Jeni and Salleé were both involved in sports from very young ages. Jeni was a dancer! She did both jazz and ballet. Salleé loved playing basketball and golf. Our love of sports continued to show as we grew older. Salleé played collegiate golf, and Jeni led group fitness classes. Through these experiences, we have had coaches foster and grow us in our skills as athletes. Our best coaches have helped us to grow in our abilities, to work as a team, to persevere in our growth even though it's hard, and to see the big picture.

Within our roles as technology coaches, we strive to be like the coaches we loved while in sports. We work with our teachers to help them grow in their abilities, work as a team, persevere, and see the big picture. We wrote this book to help coach you as you hone your skills as a teacher in this new modern classroom. We have three main goals in writing this: to empower students and teachers, to highlight the need for equitable and accessible classrooms for all learners, and to share technology and lesson ideas to maximize these efforts.

Salleé's dad was always involved in helping her grow as an athlete. Before each golf tournament, Frank would sit down with her and help her analyze each hole. We would mark the trouble areas on the card and strategize clubs and shot placements for each hole. As she played each hole, Frank observed and took notes during the tournaments. In the car ride home after the tournament, they would walk through each shot on each hole and discuss the stroke, the club choice, and the strategy. Taking time to coach Salleé through her thoughts and actions before and after a round of golf was instrumental in helping her grow as a player. It taught her to think more clearly while in play. She was able to learn from mistakes, strategize more effectively, and adjust her swing with accuracy.

This is exactly what we hope to accomplish with this book. We want to provide a coach's manual to you that will help you before, during, and after your lessons. We hope it will help you plan, analyze, and strategize how to best empower your students.

During this time of blended learning, our district utilized Microsoft Teams as a hub of learning. Our kindergarten through fifth grade students used Teams as their learning management platform, and the sixth through twelfth grade teachers used Teams Meetings to communicate and meet with their students.

We want to share with teachers ideas we learned while using Teams. Hopefully these ideas will help you navigate a digital teaching world in which there may be future instances of in-person, online, or hybrid learning—or even a mixture of all of them. We want to empower you with tools, ideas, and pedagogy to help your students learn in new and exciting ways.

To do this, we created a coach's manual for you. Our intent is to coach you in leveraging technology to equalize the playing field for your students. In turn, this will empower your classroom to use Microsoft Teams to create an accessible and equitable learning environment. The game we are coaching you for is school. The teachers are the coaches, and the students are the players. The object of the game is for the players to acquire new skills, to develop and maximize their strengths, and to apply these skills in becoming changemakers. We have broken down the manual into four parts:

> **PART 1: HUDDLE UP AND SURVEY THE FIELD** introduces you to your coaches and the modern classroom. What does this classroom look like, and what do teachers need to focus on when it comes to pedagogy and technology?

> **PART 2: DEFINING THE GAME RULES: BEST PRACTICES** gives you a tour of Microsoft Teams, with quick video explanations of how Teams works. In addition, you can see our suggestions for best practices when using Microsoft Teams in the classroom.

PART 3: **LEARN THE PLAYS** is where we share lesson ideas, templates, resources, and more. All of the edtech Teams plays you could ask for are in this section. Use them, share them, and enjoy seeing your students engaged and excited about learning and collaborating.

PART 4: **PRACTICE MAKES PERFECT** challenges you to fine-tune your teaching skills *and* your coaching skills as you prepare to coach others to use Teams in the future. We share information for you to get connected with the Microsoft family of educators, collaborate, learn, and practice putting the Teams plays into action.

How to Use This Book

This is your coach's manual. You as the teacher are the coach in your classroom. We want you to learn the best way that fits you! Mark it up, bookmark your favorite plays, highlight the pedagogy that speaks to you, or get out your phone and scan away!

As you read this book, you will find practical ways to use Teams in the classroom. Our personal learning experiences helped to generate best practices for you to implement with your students as you teach with Teams. Not only that, but you will also see lesson ideas incorporating different ways for you to empower your learners to authentically connect, collaborate, and learn in the classroom. (You do *not* have to be a Teams user to use these lessons. Many of these lessons can be applied to other platforms, such as Google Classroom or another similar LMS.)

Keep your eyes open throughout the book for these extra help segments:

Scan codes throughout this manual to access videos, templates, lesson plans, new updates, learning resources, and more! As you read this book, many of the applications we mention will have experienced many updates and may look completely different or offer new uses. Keep an eye out for QR codes that will give you access to the latest updates and newest features for each of the tools shared throughout the book.

See pro tips from Jenallee and many other exceptional educators and edtech power users from around the world. These quotes and tips will equip you to keep going and perfect your coaching skills.

Stop for a moment to reflect, evaluate, and learn more. In sports we take a time out to receive further direction, evaluate our progress, and change our approach. Throughout the book, we provide you with Time Outs to offer further explanation and direction and time for you to reflect on and evaluate your teaching practices.

In the end, we hope these tips are practical, helpful, and timeless as you work in a "new norm" of education that will continually evolve—with or without a pandemic. Education isn't the same today as it was five years ago or even one year ago. Teachers can't teach the way they always did; they have to learn new game rules, practice, and apply their new learnings. (Isn't that what they ask of their students?)

We are excited for you and hope you fall in love with Microsoft Teams as much as we have. We believe with a little coaching, a clearly defined rulebook, a good playbook, and some practice, you can provide this opportunity to your students. This is what *The Microsoft Teams Playbook* is all about.

Thank you for joining us on this journey. Tighten your laces and get hydrated as we take the next step to learn more. We hope that as you learn, you will pay it forward and share that learning with others and with us.

PART ONE

Huddle Up
and
Survey the Field

CHAPTER 1

Meet Your Coaches

When it comes to integrating technology into the classroom, we sincerely believe it is not about the technology; it is about *pedagogy* and *people*. Integrating technology is about teaching with sound pedagogy while also making authentic connections with people. As teachers, we connect with every student, finding ways to bring about authentic learning opportunities for each individual child in our classrooms.

As edtech coaches, we see firsthand that connecting and building relationships with people is how we learn. We want to learn new concepts, explore ideas, and problem-solve alongside our colleagues and fellow educators around the world. We are connected and want to learn from each other. We rely on each other, and we have a shared passion for empowering students. Through these connections, we see these extraordinary humans as our friends, collaborators, and family. This culture is embraced and fostered within the Microsoft Educator community. This community of educators exudes these traits and seeks to equip and support each other as we learn and grow together to become the best educators we can be. Microsoft Innovative Educators (MIEs) rally together online at education.microsoft.com. This hub offers educators courses on technology and pedagogy, technology tutorials, and connections with fellow educators. Through this program, Microsoft also encourages educators who are active in the community and who are creating content, leading professional development, helping the community, and so forth to apply to become Microsoft Innovative Educator Experts (MIE Experts). As MIE Experts, we have the ability to join together on monthly calls with educators across the United States that are using Microsoft every day in their classrooms. In addition to the group of MIE Experts, we have MIE Fellows leading each area/cohort in the United States. Within these cohorts, we collaborate, problem solve, and connect with MIEs in our area. This community of educators is active not only in the United States but across the globe. We value learning from MIE Experts around the world! We connect on social media and at in-person events! This community is the best personal learning network (PLN) we have ever been involved in. We truly are family seeking to lift each other up, support, collaborate, and learn together. We are honored to be MIE Experts and to have served as MIE Expert Fellows.

Many other educational technology companies have communities of educators that join together to share, learn, and support each other as well. These communities are many times fostered within ambassador programs. This means that educators can apply and join these communities as ambassadors to help and connect with fellow educators using these applications. In addition to being a part of the Microsoft family, we are also ambassadors for Wakelet, Buncee, Genially, Flipgrid, Whiteboard.chat, Beedle, and Adobe. Connecting with and serving in these amazing communities has enriched our lives as educators. We have learned much about the applications, how to use them in the classroom, and how others are using them to empower their students to do more than they were able to do before. Our experiences and the connections we have made have helped shape us into the educators we are today.

Before we go on, we want to tell you a bit about ourselves as individuals and how "Jenallee" came to be.

Jeni

My twenty-plus-year career as an educator began in 1999 when I took a position as a computer lab manager in a private school in Michigan after earning a Bachelor of Science in interdisciplinary studies from Texas A&M Commerce. But my teacher education actually began when I was a young child watching my mom. She was an amazing educator who poured her heart and soul into everything she did as a teacher. I couldn't have asked for a better role model to show me what true selfless teaching is!

Although the computer lab position was the catalyst that sparked my love for technology integration, I spent several years teaching fourth through sixth grades at a Montessori school, immersing myself in Montessori certification, and teaching sixth and seventh grade math after moving back to Texas, before I turned my attention back to technology specifically. I had been teaching in a tech-inspired classroom, but I desired to do more with technology. In the early 2000s, the role of instructional technology specialist (ITS) became extremely popular, and I began to pursue an ITS position.

I served as a tech coach at two schools in the north Texas area, where I supported teachers with tech integration, led campus and district trainings, and was instrumental in a tech rollout of laptops being used as textbooks, working to maximize the potential of these devices. Through these positions, I realized tech integration was my passion, and I decided to pursue a master's in technology integration.

A job change for my husband took us to a small town in east Tennessee, where I landed in a Microsoft district, serving as a seventh through twelfth grade English Language Arts (ELA) curriculum specialist, technology integration specialist, and science curriculum specialist. Not only did this experience increase my understanding of curriculum design, but it also allowed me to create a professional development plan for each school and staff member. Additionally, I was again an integral part of a 1:1 tech rollout and was able to teach, train, and support the teachers, students, and parents as they embarked on a digital conversion.

A final move back to Texas brought me to Eagle Mountain-Saginaw ISD, where I currently serve as a technology trainer. In this role, I have the freedom and flexibility to create a professional development plan to teach and train staff and students to use technology more efficiently to produce greater outcomes than could be done otherwise.

Salleé

I also grew up as a teacher's kid and saw the effort, care, tears, and late nights my mother, Connie Lott, poured into her work as a teacher, curriculum director, and elementary school principal. Unlike Jeni, however, seeing this picture of devotion, care, and love sent me running in the opposite direction; I wanted to be as far away from a career in education as I could get! I earned a Bachelor of Business Administration degree with a marketing major.

Ironically, during my final year of undergraduate studies, I began subbing at my mother's school to earn extra income and, as I began my first day on the job, I knew *this* was where I was supposed to be! I loved seeing the students laugh, learn, and glow with excitement as I introduced new concepts. After many hours of discussion about changing my major, I took the advice to remain in my BBA degree plan and become alternatively certified.

In 2005, I was hired as a pre-kindergarten general education and special education teacher. During this time I was mentored by some amazing educators and administrators who helped me develop quality teaching strategies and classroom management skills. I went on to earn a Master of Science in Educational Technology and a librarian certification, and then, for six years, I incorporated my love of learning and technology into the Aubrey ISD library program as a district librarian.

While serving in this role, my husband's job transferred us to the Forth Worth area, where I served as a librarian and where my passions became clear and concise. Again, I had amazing mentors who encouraged me to use my creativity and outside-the-box thinking to transform the library into a media center rich in technology. I led professional developments on campus, in the district, and at state conferences. With one-to-one technology, blogging, and collaborative projects, I found myself using technology to empower students to learn, chase their passions, and change their mindsets. I planned technology-rich lessons with teachers, using the resources available within the district, and was given the flexibility to co-teach, flip lessons, and design STEM (science, technology, education, and math) activities.

As I was leaning into my newfound vision and passion for empowering students through technology, my friends at Eagle Mountain-Saginaw ISD informed me of upcoming openings in the instructional technology department. I was blessed to be hired into one of the two vacancies, with Jeni being hired into the other.

Jenallee

As we taught, trained, and learned together, a deep friendship and sisterhood developed. We have learned to encourage each other and help each other become the best instructional technologists we can be. One thing we did that was especially helpful was a self-assessment when our team read Gallup's *StrengthFinders 2.0* a few years ago. Through this book and related strengths evaluation, we discovered our personal strengths, learned about each other's strengths, and learned to leverage those strengths to benefit our teachers and students.

Jeni's general strengths are in the area of relating to and influencing others and executing tasks, and they are evident in her leading with a smile and positivity and through her upbeat demeanor. She is also the one who makes sure the calendar is up to date, sending Salleé reminders to get things done by due dates.

Salleé has relating strengths but also has strategic strengths. She shines a light on the positive side of situations and cares deeply for others, empathizing with their pain and needs. She connects with people on a deeper level in conversations and is quick to develop ideas and strategies for implementing projects.

Our strengths complement each other nicely. We both like people and are both positive. However, Salleé is strategic while Jeni is strong in execution. This enables us to help each other and makes our work more productive and enjoyable. We are also more efficient with our time. Together we make a greater impact on learning. We can connect with teachers, bring ideas for teaching concepts, and be strategic in our execution of campus, school, and global projects. Together we are better, so we became "Jenallee."

Creating instructional videos and how-to documents became a common Jenallee task, but we knew more was needed. Teachers across each of our campuses continually asked the same questions, and we began to wonder how we could reach more teachers in a timely, fun, and effective manner. What about a YouTube channel? On March 1, 2018, we recorded our first "Jenallee" video with Sarah Mullins, an English teacher from Saginaw High School.

Check out this video here.

Jenallee knew if one teacher had a specific question, others had the same one, so we began to go into classrooms and interview teachers to offer solutions to those questions so many teachers across the district (and across the world) had. These videos were shared on Facebook and YouTube and, over time, we formed deep friendships with many in the district and also across the globe.

We love being "Jenallee." We are teachers and best friends! Also, we "eat and breathe" teaching and empowering our students and teachers with the best learning opportunities possible. We want to help you see yourself honestly as an educator, maximize your students' learning potential, and infuse your lessons with technology to empower your students to do more than they have done before! We would love to connect with you! We grow from our PLN, and we would love to learn with you!

Scan this QR code to connect with us!

Our Journey with Teams

We began using Microsoft Teams in 2018, as it was making its educational debut. As tech enthusiasts, we wanted to see what this learning management platform had to offer. We found that it filled the gaps in helping our students connect and collaborate as they learned. Microsoft Teams is a learning hub that offers teachers the ability to share learning resources while also fostering student-driven learning with features such as chat, posts, assignments, and meetings. We explored, experimented, and tried to use all of its features. We went into classrooms and used it with teachers, we made videos for our teachers and our PLN, and we shared our knowledge on podcasts and more.

Scan this QR code to hear from Jeff Bradbury, an educator, speaker and broadcaster with Teacher Cast, and Jenallee, as we share how we began using Microsoft Teams.

Scan this QR code to meet your coaches, Jeni and Salleé.

CHAPTER 2

Home Field Advantage

In the preface, we shared a bit about our *Why*. We are children of educators who feel called to empower students to do more. Our own children have made us passionate about equipping *all* students with the technology they need to own their learning! Solidifying our *Why* has been key to understanding our motivations, mission, and strengths as educators.

* What is your **Why**?

* Why are you a teacher?

* What aspects of your background and experiences helped you develop your why?

Our experiences in life and as teachers—before and during the pandemic—solidified the first thing educators need to do. It isn't mind-blowing or novel, and it isn't a new pedagogy. No matter what kind of classroom you teach, the most important aspect of your job is to build relationships. In fact, we bet a relationship with someone is part of your *Why*. Maybe your family or a friend—or even a student—influenced your reason to teach. *People* are important, and quality education begins with relationships.

* Who influenced you to become a teacher?

We bet you can guess who influenced us. Yep, our moms!

Scan this QR code to check out our Jenallee interview with our moms about education!

Home Field Advantage

In sports, having the home field advantage means being the team that is in a familiar place and knows most of the fans watching them play. They are comfortable and enthusiastically supported, and they may perform better than their opponent because of this advantage.

In the classroom, the teacher has the home field advantage. You have the opportunity to know every single one of your students in a way that no one else does. You have the most insight into your students' interests, data, and performance trends. You also know how the "game of school" is played in your classroom. You know the uniqueness of your classroom—where the bumps are and how to win in this space.

Ultimately, because of this advantage, you have the opportunity to help each of your students develop their skills within this space. By taking time to get to know them, you can leverage your knowledge to maximize their learning in the classroom.

Building Relationships with Your Students

Building relationships is the first step in honing your homefield advantage. As a librarian, Salleé enjoyed using books as a way to connect with students. When she saw a student reading a book about dogs, she would begin asking questions to connect with the student, such as, do you have a dog? Or what is your favorite breed of dog? The next time that student returned to the library, Salleé would have a book waiting for them that connected to their responses. This was a way to help that student know that they were important, they were heard, and they had a connection with their teacher.

Time Out

* How do you cultivate an environment where your students feel welcomed, comfortable, safe, and willing to take risks?

* How do you include the different languages, abilities, cultures, strengths, and interests of all of your learners in the learning environment?

As education continues to change, cultivating deep relationships with your students is more important than ever. The following activities are some we have used to initiate connection with our students.

- *Interest Inventory.* On the first day of school, give students a piece of paper (or personally interview them) to write down or draw pictures of things they are most interested in.
- *Scavenger Hunt.* Create a "get to know each other" scavenger hunt, where students have to ask each other questions to "find" the traits they're hunting for.
- *Get to Know Your Teacher.* Create a Flipgrid topic to share five things about yourself. Give students the opportunity to ask you questions or tell one thing they have in common with you.
- *Get to Know Your Students.* Ask parents or guardians to write you a letter about their child. Include a prompt for them to share interests and hobbies as well as personality traits and other things they may want you to know about their child.

I (Jeni) loved asking my students' parents to write letters about their children. After a few weeks of school, I would read them again and reflect on who each student was and how they learned. These letters opened my eyes to things I may not have seen solely through my "teacher lens." For instance, in the case of our personal children, would I (Salleé) have known Hunter

needed to express his thoughts graphically instead of in written form? Would I (Jeni) have known Payton needed to sit near the teacher and would need frequent check-ins because she might not raise her hand for help or speak up, and might easily slip through the cracks unnoticed?

Those letters really helped me understand my students from a different perspective and usually helped me connect necessary dots. Building relationships with your students from the beginning is so important. If you want to build trust and a good rapport with them, they need to know you genuinely care about them.

As moms, we value the connection teachers make with our kids. The little things often make a huge impact on our kids and on us. For example, Hunter received a Ramen noodle sweatshirt and matching sweatpants for Christmas. It was one "loud" outfit, and Hunter *loved* it! It was not glamorous, but it was all the rage among ninth grade boys! Hunter's gymnastics coach had noticed his excitement and joy over his Ramen sweatshirt. While eating lunch one day in the lounge, his coach spotted an extra package of spicy noodles and gave it to Hunter as a gift. This small, thoughtful action made Hunter's day; he felt special and important.

Does this have anything to do with Hunter's education? Absolutely! This teacher connected with him and communicated that he was important. Because of this, Hunter will be more willing to work for him, listen to him, and invest in what he says. As an educator, your job is to invest in your students, get to know them, and find ways to connect to them. If you don't know *all* your students, how can you offer them an equitable learning experience? How will you know what drives them to learn? How will you know how to craft relevant lessons?

Are You Watching or Playing?

In 2016, Katrena Perou, then Chief Program Officer at the Urban Arts Partnership, shared in a TEDx Talk an inspirational story of the importance of Maslow's Hierarchy of needs. Perou shared how she discovered the importance of meeting students' needs to build relationships in a quest to empower student voice through their personal passion, music.

In her talk, Katrena explained her role in this nonprofit organization was to work with students in underprivileged schools to advance their academic and artistic development. To prepare, she worked to understand each school she served, including the dangers, fears, and risks these students faced every day.

In one school, where only 29.6 percent of the students graduated, Katrena studied the students and found one aspect they were all excited about: music. Together the students and Katrena produced a music CD that essentially spoke for the students. Listening to the students express their needs through the lyrics of their writings enabled Katrena to connect with them and, ultimately, help them to share their voice. Their voice showed that their needs needed to be met before learning could occur. As educators we have learned from Abraham Maslow that if certain needs are not met, students cannot learn. Physiological needs, safety, belonging, and self-esteem all must be met before self-actualization and inner pursuit of learning can occur. For Katrena, the lyrics in the students' songs gave her a glimpse into their needs. She was able to see that they were not sleeping well and did not feel safe, two of the bottom layers of Maslow's pyramid.

Katrena says working with students requires doing three things in a specific order: *listening*, *building trust*, and *helping*. Listening to your students assures them you are trustworthy. As you build trust with your students, you can then begin to truly help them.

By listening, Katrena learned the students were missing key components of Maslow's Pyramid. Without these, they were not able to learn effectively. The song lyrics showed Karena that her students were not getting their physiological and safety needs met. Without these needs being met, her students were going to have a hard time learning.

How did she build trust with her students? Katrena was a college basketball player. She shared the analogy of how she would study her opponents on the court. She does the same for the students in her program. So, she studied the competition. She wanted to know what was keeping the students from attending her after-school program. What was more intriguing to them? Then she brought these aspects into her program.

Through listening, building trust, and relating to her students, she was able to help them. She knew what their needs were, she studied how to connect with them, and then she met their needs to bring them to self-actualization and learning.

At the end of her TEDx Talk, Katrena used an analogy we really like. She asks her audience whether they are in the stands *watching* the game or on the team *playing* the game? She says it is easy for those in the stands to judge the players and *talk* about what needs to happen. By *playing* the game, you can *make* things happen!

As teachers we can sit in the stands, look at our students and see what they are doing wrong. We can critique them and tell them what they should be doing. That is easy. The players hear the people in the stands, but they listen to the coach. The coach is the one who knows the players' strengths and needs. When we teachers join the game as coaches, we can begin to make things happen. As coaches, we build relationships with the students, we meet their needs, and we coach them in becoming the best players they can be. By playing the game, you can make things happen!

To view Katrena's entire TEDx Talk, scan this QR code.

Time Out

* As you consider your role as a teacher, are you watching in the stands or are you playing the game? What is your evidence?

* How are you listening to your students and building their trust so you can help them be better learners?

By taking these actions, you can construct the home field advantage for each of your students as well. As you learn their needs, you can build lessons relevant for them. In turn, they will be comfortable and feel supported and will be able to perform their best!

Coaches' Corner

Something we have done to help us learn about our students is keep track of our findings. We have discovered this data is just as important as the test scores we keep in our data binders. Create a learner profile—a player stat card—to document your research about each of your students. For each student, you may want to note the following:

- Specific needs
- Background
- Interests
- Data
- Trends
- Goals

Use these stats to craft a home field advantage for each student—offering relevant lessons with accessible and differentiated content. Your understanding of your students and purposeful planning will allow you to craft relevant lessons students can easily connect to.

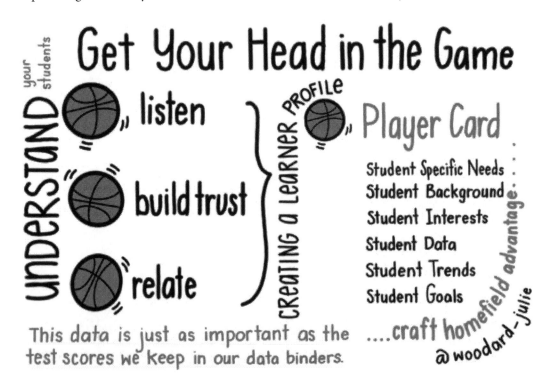

Use the template found in this QR code to create a player's card for each of your students. Then simply add it to your digital data binder or physical data binder. We've included a sample.

* Before we move on, take a look at the response you jotted down earlier and consider this question again: *How do you cultivate an environment where your students feel welcomed, comfortable, safe, and willing to take risks?* Is there anything you would add or change about how you cultivate such an environment?

* *What is your game plan for studying your students and the competition? What are your students' strengths? What is drawing their attention away from learning?*

CHAPTER 3

Level the Playing Field

"Good morning, Gretchen!"

"Hi, Ms. Long. I brought you a scone."

"Why, thank you! I needed that today. I didn't get my breakfast this morning!" "*Buenos dias,* Juan. How are you?"

"*Bien!*"

"Ms. Clark, you look pretty today."

"Well, thank you, Peng. You look very pretty today as well. And, Charlie, how are you today? It's so nice to see you."

[No response]

"Charlie, did you see the big game last night?"

[No response]

Each morning you stand at your door and greet your students—students with unique needs, challenges, and abilities. And your job is to teach every one of them—not just the "straight A" students or the engaged, independent learners. You can level the playing field so all your students—every Payton and Hunter in your class—can learn in the ways that are best for them. You can offer an equitable classroom. You can know each of them personally, advocate for them, and coach them as they need to be the best they can be.

Your charge as teachers is to empower each of your students! In an ideal classroom, this would be easy; in a realistic classroom, it can be difficult. You may have 150 students demanding your attention, help, and time. You need to make individual accommodations while also making sure everyone is meeting the testing data minimum. How can you do it all?

What Is a Level Playing Field?

A lot of factors go into playing the game of school. Some of these you, as the teacher, can control—many of them you cannot. In this section, we are talking only about what you *can* control within your classroom to help every one of your students. When we say, "level the playing field," we mean providing each student with what she needs to do her best in the game; we do not mean the *same* for every student. We mean for teachers to give every student what he needs individually to succeed.

Some may say, "That is not fair," and believe if students aren't given things equally, some are getting an advantage. But we see it differently. We don't believe "fair" looks the same for every student. To us, "fair" is giving each student what she needs. This is what puts all students on the same playing field with the same opportunity to learn. In this situation, all students have what they need to access content, create, and be passionate about learning.

Cultivating an Equitable Classroom

We believe technology in the classroom is the power that provides all students with an accessible and equitable learning opportunity. Technology levels the playing field for your students. Ken Shelton—educator, educational technology specialist, and ISTE Digital Equity PLN 2018 Excellence Award winner—uses the term *techquity* to describe the role technology plays in making classrooms more equitable. In *The Chromebook Infused Classroom*, Holly Clark notes Shelton explains that techquity is the "dynamic combination of access to technology and the rich information that brings greater equity to all students regardless of race, gender, ethnicity, or socioeconomic status." Real equity exists when we begin to merge the use of educational technologies with culturally responsive and relevant learning experiences to support student development and essential skills.

Technology brings equity and accessibility to the classroom. It offers all stakeholders—parents, students, teachers, community, and the global audience—a unified location for learning with current resources at their fingertips. Without technology, only individuals physically in the same location could learn and collaborate, and resources would be outdated as soon as they were printed. Technology offers teachers the ability to make relevant learning experiences accessible to all students.

We believe technology is the answer. But educational technology offers so many excellent applications. How do you know where to start to leverage technology's power to level the playing field in your classroom? Many people look to a learning management system (LMS), and there are many great options to choose from. As MIE Experts, Microsoft Trainers, and educators who work for a Microsoft school district, you can likely guess which LMS application we prefer. You are correct! Microsoft Teams.

We especially like Teams because, as our friend Justin Chando, principal head of design of Flipgrid at Microsoft, says, "Teams is not an LMS; it is so much more!" We wouldn't even label Teams as an LMS. Instead, a "learning ecosystem" is more fitting. This term was coined by Emily Ewining, one of our EMS ISD fifth grade students in Mrs. Jennifer Anders's class.

In her Teams post, Emily explained she views Teams as an ecosystem because the system continually evolved and changed as students added posts and content! Yes, Emily! This is the perfect way to describe Teams. It is not an LMS or a conference center. It is an ecosystem where people can share, plan, collaborate, and create together. This is the type of environment we want our students to learn in. We want them to listen to each other, speak words of truth and kindness, share their "aha" moments, feel safe to ask questions, and see the classroom as a space to explore, learn, and safely fail. Teams fosters this environment. It is an ecosystem that thrives on conversations and collaborations. We want to show you how you can harness the power of Microsoft Teams to make the classroom an enjoyable learning environment where you can efficiently

and effectively facilitate learning, maximizing accessibility and equability for all. Every student, regardless of ability, struggles, or situation, will have access to content and the ability to learn within a relevant and meaningful classroom. We want your classroom to be a healthy ecosystem where your students enjoy learning and thrive.

Making Your Classroom Accessible for All

Teams makes learning accessible to students through Microsoft Learning Tools. Microsoft Learning Tools are tools that are built into Microsoft products. These tools include Immersive Reader, Dictation, Inking, and more. These tools enable students to listen to content read aloud, dictate their thoughts, see images for unfamiliar words, translate content, and much more. As Mike Tholfsen, Principal Group Product Manager—Microsoft Education, says, these tools offer every student a "non-stigmatizing, free, built-in, and mainstream" learning environment. These tools have been life-changing for Payton and Hunter. By using these tools, they have been able to own their learning. Their learning is not hindered by lack of access; it is championed by tools that support their individual needs.

Accessibility tools can help level the playing field for your students; however, technology can't fully equalize learning without the teacher. The teacher has the homefield advantage and the power to construct an equitable and accessible learning environment for every student. We have examined this concept through our teacher, mom, special education, and edtech lenses and identified five areas where teachers can use technology to offer an equal learning environment for every child in the classroom:

1. Student agency
2. Relevancy
3. Accessibility
4. Assessment

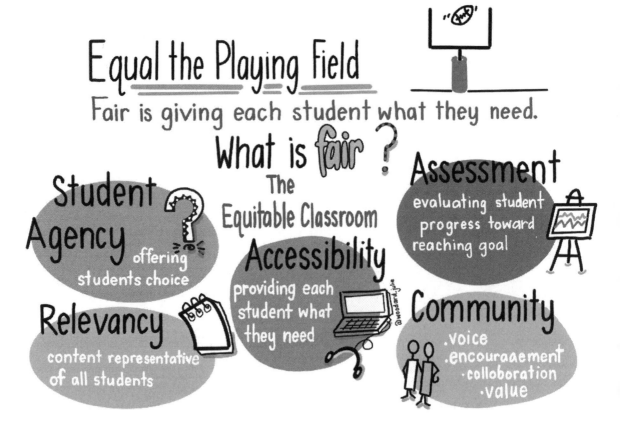

We then specifically looked at how we can offer this service to our students through blended instruction using Microsoft Teams.

Student Agency

Student agency is offering students choice in what they learn and how they learn it. We believe every student deserves to see relevant problems, explore solutions, and passionately present solutions to an authentic audience. Driving their own learning gives students the unique opportunity to see how they can make substantial changes within their current environment. Trevor Mackenzie explains student agency eloquently in his book *The Inquiry Mindset*:

> Although it's important we ask our students how they would like to demonstrate their learning, student agency is about so much more. It requires educators to hold themselves accountable to values they must embody and intentionally work towards.

The values include genuine decision-making, the learner knowing his or her strengths and stretches, opportunity to explore passions in school, student questions that shape their learning, and showing learning in different ways.

Educators need to build relationships with students and plan lessons in which risks and genuine learning opportunities are plausible. Not every learning moment will result in a profound change in society, but these moments may likely make a profound change in the learner.

Put It into Practice

How can you put student agency into practice? You can offer students choice about how they learn and how they visualize their thinking. One of our favorite teachers, Starr Lara, made this real for us by the way she responded to Hunter's submission of an assigned written essay with specific criteria. For Hunter, a document with text was boring and hard; he wanted to make it interesting by creating a PowerPoint presentation.

She evaluated his work and saw he had included all of the items required for the essay. She praised Hunter for his work and realized he needed creative ways to express his thoughts and learning. Could she have quickly responded and given Hunter a zero for his work? Absolutely. Would this have crushed him? Absolutely. Instead, she encouraged this timid learner who struggles with dyslexia to learn and visually express his learning in a way that best fit him. Because she knew him, she was able to allow his learning journey to be exciting and fun and to result in a proud learning moment for this scholar. We were so impressed with Hunter's work and with Ms. Lara's eagerness to encourage Hunter's creative learning style. This is a perfect example of building student agency. Ms. Lara knew Hunter, and she encouraged him to learn and express his learning in his own way, while ensuring he was learning the required content.

Time Out

Teachers want their students to own their learning. This means that students will intrinsically seek after solutions to relevant problems and bring their learning and solutions to an authentic audience. This offers students the ability to make an impact with their learning. Teachers want their students to be changemakers who are passionate about life and seek solutions to benefit the world. By fostering student agency, you inspire these changemakers.

One of the best ways we have built student agency into our lessons is by creating HyperDocs to walk students through the lesson cycle. With a HyperDoc, you can . . .

- engage learners with previous knowledge
- explore driving questions
- directly teach concepts
- apply knowledge
- reflect on learning

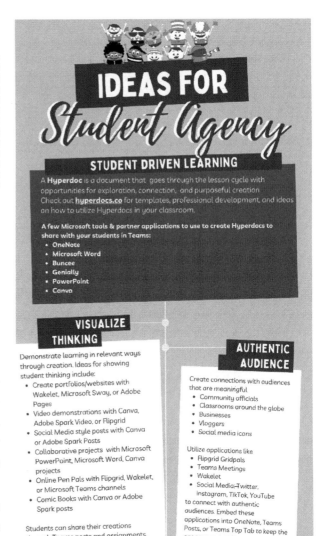

IDEAS FOR
Student Agency

STUDENT DRIVEN LEARNING

A **Hyperdoc** is a document that goes through the lesson cycle with opportunities for exploration, connection, and purposeful creation. Check out **hyperdocs.co** for templates, professional development, and ideas on how to utilize Hyperdocs in your classroom.

A few Microsoft tools & partner applications to use to create Hyperdocs to share with your students in Teams:
- OneNote
- Microsoft Word
- Buncee
- Genially
- PowerPoint
- Canva

VISUALIZE THINKING

Demonstrate learning in relevant ways through creation. Ideas for showing student thinking include:
- Create portfolios/websites with Wakelet, Microsoft Sway, or Adobe Pages
- Video demonstrations with Canva, Adobe Spark Video, or Flipgrid
- Social Media style posts with Canva or Adobe Spark Posts
- Collaborative projects with Microsoft PowerPoint, Microsoft Word, Canva projects
- Online Pen Pals with Flipgrid, Wakelet, or Microsoft Teams channels
- Comic Books with Canva or Adobe Spark posts

Students can share their creations through Teams posts and assignments.

AUTHENTIC AUDIENCE

Create connections with audiences that are meaningful
- Community officials
- Classrooms around the globe
- Businesses
- Vloggers
- Social media icons

Utilize applications like
- Flipgrid Gridpals
- Teams Meetings
- Wakelet
- Social Media–Twitter, instagram, TikTok, YouTube
to connect with authentic audiences. Embed these applications into OneNote, Teams Posts, or Teams Top Tab to keep the engagement within student reach.

QUESTIONING

We want our students to develop and ask questions! Some digital ideas for generating thoughtful conversations and questions include:

- KWL chart in Whiteboard.chat
- AEIOU Discovery Education
- Formative assessments with Quizlet, Quizizz, Kahoot, Blooket, Forms, or OneNote

Scan here for digital access to interactive links

KNOWING STRENGTHS

Discover student strengths with various polling and self-evaluation activities. Use Teams Posts to share quizzes with your students.

Genius Hour
Students explore their strengths, encourage each other in their strengths, and explore their passions.

Strength Finders
Quiz students can take to determine their top 3 strengths. Students see their own strengths and their peers. They can begin to understand and rely on each other's strengths.

Personality Quizzes
Personality quizzes that help identify student strengths.

With Teams and HyperDocs, all students have content accessible to them and are able to drive their learning. They explore content and formalize their thoughts to answer the driving question. Students share their reflections, thoughts, and questions to inform teachers in their instruction. Students apply their knowledge through a demonstration of learning they choose and, finally, reflect on their understanding of the driving question and set learning goals as they justify their learning.

Coaches' Corner

Scan this QR code to see a #Jenallee interview with Lisa Highfill, c authors of *The HyperDoc Handbook,* and Holly Clark, author of *The Microsoft Infused Classroom,* about HyperDocs.

Relevancy

All students deserve learning opportunities that are relevant to them—relevant to their personal culture, language, and interests and also to modern events and content representative of all students. Through building relationships with your students, you will know which of these factors need to be woven into your curriculum and lessons to enable you to create driving questions that intrigue. By doing this, you can ensure every child is engaged, connected, and empowered by your lessons. *This* makes learning equitable.

Children need to see books and explore content about people who look like them, sound like them, and have the same experiences as them. Connect content to different cultures, languages, modern events, and student interests within the class. Make sure to focus on all cultural triumphs within your classroom. Again, this boils down to you knowing your students and developing learning experiences that connect with the students in the classroom. Remember, you have the home field advantage. You know how to make learning relevant to your students because you have a relationship with them.

Knowing your students means knowing about their culture, language, relatable modern events, and student interests. After building relationships with your students and learning about who they are generally, educate yourself on these specific factors as well. This will benefit you as you develop content that is relevant to all students.

Scan this QR code for a curated list of resources to help you craft relevant lessons for your classroom.

Accessibility

Every student in the classroom should have equal access to content. Again, *equal* does not mean the *same*. Equal means providing each student with what she needs. You may have students who need content read aloud; others may need high-contrast backgrounds to be able to see content. Some students may need to dictate responses rather than writing them down.

Teams technology provides access to content in a non-stigmatizing environment, built into the technology. It is mainstream—and *free*. Learning Tools offers every student the ability to own his learning, and the technology affords *all* students the ability to access content that equalizes the playing field.

Some educators may strongly advocate traditional teaching methods. They may not see the need for Microsoft Learning Tools or may even see it as an easy way out of learning or even as cheating. Instead, we hope that you can see the power in *all* students accessing content with these technology tools. Students are empowered when they can choose how they want to learn, write, and create, and Teams makes this possible by putting the tools at their fingertips. For many students, these tools are life-changing and will replace the traditional tools and methods educators hold dear.

Differentiation is another part of making content accessible to all students, and you can use Teams to differentiate instruction as needed. You can modify assignments and send them to specific students. You can create channels with scaffolded content and create private channels for students to work and ask questions in. You can also meet with students through Teams Meetings to demonstrate concepts and provide support.

To give you an "at a glance" resource for Microsoft Learning Tools, we have provided the availability chart below:

Microsoft Learning Tools Availability

	OneNote Desktop	OneNote Web	OneNote App	OneNote iOS	OneNote Mac	Word Web	Word Desktop	Word Mac	Word iPad	PowerPoint Web	Outlook Web	Outlook Desktop	Teams	Flipgrid Web iOS Android	Whiteboard	Forms	OneDrive + SharePoint	MakeCode	Minecraft EDU	Office Lens iOS Android	Edge browser
Read Aloud & word/line highlighting	OneNote Desktop	OneNote Web	OneNote App	OneNote iOS	OneNote Mac	Word Web	Word Desktop	Word Mac	Word iPad	PowerPoint Web	Outlook Web	Outlook Desktop	Teams	Flipgrid Web iOS Android	Whiteboard	Forms	OneDrive + SharePoint	MakeCode	Minecraft EDU	Office Lens iOS Android	Edge browser
Spacing and Font Size	OneNote Desktop	OneNote Web	OneNote App	OneNote iOS	OneNote Mac	Word Web	Word Desktop	Word Mac	Word iPad	PowerPoint Web	Outlook Web		Teams	Flipgrid Web iOS Android	Whiteboard	Forms	OneDrive + SharePoint	MakeCode	Minecraft EDU	Office Lens iOS Android	Edge browser
Page Colors	OneNote Desktop	OneNote Web	OneNote App	OneNote iOS	OneNote Mac	Word Web	Word Desktop	Word Mac		PowerPoint Web	Outlook Web		Teams	Flipgrid Web iOS Android	Whiteboard	Forms	OneDrive + SharePoint	MakeCode	Minecraft EDU	Office Lens iOS Android	Edge browser
Syllables	OneNote Desktop	OneNote Web	OneNote App	OneNote iOS	OneNote Mac	Word Web	Word Desktop	PowerPoint Web			Outlook Web		Teams	Flipgrid Web iOS Android	Whiteboard	Forms	OneDrive + SharePoint	MakeCode	Minecraft EDU	Office Lens iOS Android	Edge browser
Line Focus	OneNote Desktop	OneNote Web	OneNote App	OneNote iOS	OneNote Mac	Word Web	Word Desktop	PowerPoint			Outlook Web		Teams	Flipgrid Web iOS Android	Whiteboard	Forms	OneDrive + SharePoint	MakeCode	Minecraft EDU	Office Lens iOS Android	Edge browser
Parts of Speech	OneNote Desktop	OneNote Web	OneNote App	OneNote iOS	OneNote Mac	Word Web	PowerPoint Web	Outlook Web					Teams	Flipgrid Web iOS Android	Whiteboard	Forms	OneDrive + SharePoint	MakeCode	Minecraft EDU	Office Lens iOS Android	Edge browser
Picture Dictionary	OneNote Desktop	OneNote Web	OneNote App	OneNote iOS	OneNote Mac	Word Web	PowerPoint Web	Outlook Web					Teams	Flipgrid Web iOS Android	Whiteboard	Forms	OneDrive + SharePoint	MakeCode	Minecraft EDU	Office Lens iOS Android	Edge browser
Translation	OneNote Desktop	OneNote Web	OneNote App	OneNote iOS	OneNote Mac	Word Web	PowerPoint Web	Outlook Web					Teams	Flipgrid Web iOS Android	Whiteboard	Forms	OneDrive + SharePoint	MakeCode	Minecraft EDU	Office Lens iOS Android	Edge browser
Math & Equations	OneNote Web	OneNote App	OneNote iOS	OneNote Mac	Word Web	Word Desktop	PowerPoint Desktop	Forms	Edge browser												
Dictation	OneNote Desktop	OneNote App	OneNote Web	Word Web	Word Desktop	Outlook Desktop	PowerPoint Desktop	PowerPoint Web	Windows 10												

Learning Tools Flyer for PD: http://aka.ms/LearningToolsFlyer

Time Out

Scan this QR code to see a Jenallee interview with Mike Tholfsen, Product Manager with Microsoft EDU, where we discuss what an inclusive classroom looks like. Mike shares how Immersive Reader and Learning Tools make the classroom non-stigmatizing.

Accessibility also includes devices; every student needs equal access to devices and the internet so they can connect to content. As a result of this pandemic, many schools received technology for their students. Although this greatly narrowed the divide across the nation, not every student has a device. We encourage you to be a voice for access to devices and internet, as well as content, in your schools and communities.

Assessment

Assessment is another area in which teachers can use technology to create a level playing field. Educators have to know their students—personally and through data. Assessments help teachers better understand their students through the data. Each student is on her own personal learning journey, and assessment evaluates students' progress toward meeting specific learning goals. But assessment also involves evaluating your own teaching methods to ensure you are using the most effective methods.

Our thoughts about creating authentic assessment align with Grant Wiggins' idea of *backward design*. In the *Edutopia* article, "Grant Wiggins: Defining Assessment," he says, "One of the challenges in teaching is designing, and to be a good designer you have to think about what you're trying to accomplish and craft a combination of the content and the instructional methods, but also the assessment . . . We call it 'backward design.'"

Wiggins says that, instead of jumping right into activities because they are "cool" or fun for students, ask yourself what your objective is and then ask whether you can achieve the objective using those activities. In other words, begin with the end in mind. As Wiggins and Jay McTighe outline in *Understanding by Design*, look at your learning objectives, determine the evidence you want your students to display in an assessment, and then plan your instructional methods, lessons, and strategies.

How is technology used in this process? It can be used throughout; however, it especially comes into play as you determine the evidence you want to see and plan your methods, lessons, and strategies. We have identified four categories of digital evidence of learning that can be easily seen and displayed within Microsoft Teams:

1. **Goal Setting**—helping students individually set goals and assess their own progress over time
2. **Formative Assessment**—looking at the current knowledge of students; the teacher uses these findings to adjust their teaching and strategies to meet the overall goal
3. **Competency Based**—providing a summative assessment that displays the students' working knowledge of the concepts taught
4. **Reflection**—allowing students a space to reflect on and assess their learning

Scan this QR code to see a breakdown of each assessment evidence category and view a chart with various ideas on how to assess students with Microsoft Teams and partner applications.

Throughout the learning process in Teams, teachers can offer quality feedback for students while also assessing their own teaching methods. Taking time to reflect and offer feedback for both aspects of assessment is important for growth.

John Hattie has written many books and blogs about feedback. In his blog post, "Feedback in Schools," featured in *Visible Learning for Teachers*, Hattie says that "Feedback is one of the top 10 influences on student achievement." One of the most powerful pieces of Teams is its feedback loop. Instead of something we do only during the assessment, feedback is essential throughout the entire lesson cycle. Timely feedback is essential to help students predict and alter their work to arrive at the outcome they are seeking to meet. Teams feedback loop is a method of gathering evidence, designed to help you provide this important feedback throughout the entire learning process.

Microsoft Teams is equipped with Assignments. As the teacher, you have the ability to create assignments right from within Teams. You can use many different applications to form assignments, including OneNote, Word, PowerPoint, and Microsoft partner applications such as Buncee and Whiteboard.chat. Here is an example of one of our preferred ways to create a HyperDoc assignment in Teams and OneNote and offer feedback to students throughout the learning process. This continual feedback loop is easily achieved within Microsoft Teams.

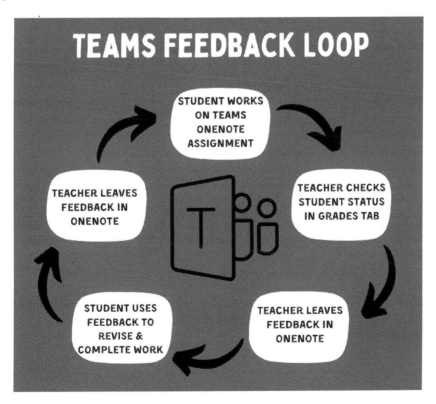

The loop works through eight basic steps:

1. Teacher creates OneNote HyperDoc assignment in Teams.
2. Student works through the lesson cycle in the Teams OneNote Notebook.
3. Teacher checks student status in the Grades tab. (Teacher can see whether student has viewed, is working, or has completed work.)
4. Teacher leaves feedback in OneNote as student completes work.
5. Student uses feedback to complete work.
6. Teacher checks finished work and returns additional feedback to student.
7. Student corrects work according to feedback.
8. Once student masters the skill, the teacher will confirm with additional feedback.

By using assessment with meaningful feedback to check for individual growth, you are equaling the playing field.

Community

As noted earlier, building relationships with your students is key; however, you can't stop there. Students need a learning environment where they are encouraged, befriended, and valued. In addition to building relationships with your students, you need to encourage and foster healthy relationships between the students in your classroom.

John Hattie speaks to this need in his book, *Visible Learning for Teachers: Maximizing Impact on Learning*:

> For many students, school can be a lonely place, and low classroom acceptance by peers can be linked with subsequent disengagement and lowered achievement. There needs to be a sense of belonging, and this can come from peers. Certainly, when a student has friends at a school, it is a different and better place. In studies looking at what happens to students when they move schools, the single greatest predictor of subsequent success is whether the students make a friend in the first month (Galton et al., 2000; Pratt and George, 2005). It is incumbent, therefore, upon schools to attend to student friendships, ensure the class welcomes newcomers, and, at minimum, ensure all students have a sense of belonging.

The culture in the classroom has a direct impact on student learning. Students need to feel valued by the teacher and their peers. Teachers need to foster a community of inclusivity, encouragement, and safety. To best foster this environment, you have to teach students how to treat each other, and you have to follow the same guidelines you set for the students.

Focus on these four aspects to build community within your classroom:

1. **Talk to each other.** Every student has a voice in the classroom. The way students and teachers speak to each other can determine a student's self-efficacy. Make it a priority to teach your students how to speak to each other and how to cultivate friendships.

2. **Encourage each other.** Everyone needs a word of encouragement. Even when you think you don't need it, you likely feel good when someone encourages you. Make it a daily habit and practice to encourage your students. The positive impact you make on your students will endure for the rest of their lives. In addition, we want our students to learn how to encourage each other. This is a lifetime skill that can be fostered and developed in your classroom.

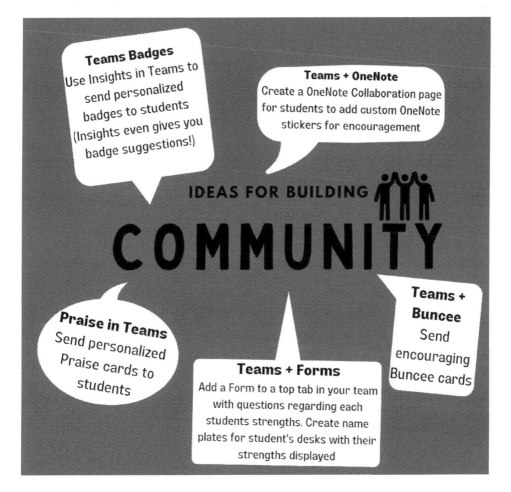

3. ***Work together.*** Being on a team and working collectively toward a common goal can be an invigorating learning experience. Fostering camaraderie, encouragement, and reliability teaches your students the splendor of teamwork.

4. ***Value each other.*** Reframing how you view others in the classroom is a great way to show you value them. For example, in our homes we have reframed the stereotypical view of dyslexia. Instead of seeing it as a disability, we see as a strength. By reframing our language at home, we can show greater value to our children. By doing the same in your learning environment, you can show greater value to your students.

You set the tone for the community within your classroom. You are the cheerleader that has the ability to unite the classroom in a chant together that is inclusive, encouraging, and positive. What is the chant or cheer you want your class to believe and say? What is the unified voice you want your students to hear and trust? What we say within the classroom influences how our students interact with each other, what they think of each other, and what they say to themselves.

Throughout their lives, your students will hear a lot of negative messages, but you have the opportunity to encourage them. In fact, with the power of a megaphone, you can speak louder than those negative messages and reinforce their inner positive voices. For the one year your students are in your class, speak loudly through your "encouragement megaphone" to boost each student's individual voice and your students' collective voice. Empower them to believe in themselves, drown out the negative voices in their path, have confidence, and take risks.

One of our favorite examples of this idea in action is from Lake Pointe Elementary School. Every morning the entire school raises their unified voice.

Scan this QR code to hear
their morning cheer.

CHAPTER 4

Getting Started with Teams

Now that you have surveyed the playing field, you are ready to play. But first, you need to learn *how* to play. Our guess is that if you had already mastered using Teams to create an equitable and accessible classroom, you wouldn't be reading this book. Perhaps you want to know more about how to use Microsoft Teams in your class, in your PLC group, or maybe with your school or the team of teachers you work with. Maybe you want to create a club or a place for students to come together to share ideas and collaborate.

This section of the book breaks down the main components of Microsoft Teams. We also offer suggestions and tips from our experiences of working with teachers and students across our district. We will briefly discuss what Teams is and how to use the basic features and then take a deeper dive into defining the game rules and identifying best practices for each of the features.

What Is Microsoft Teams?

As you know well from teaching during a pandemic, an online classroom is an important aspect of in-person, hybrid, *and* remote learning. Microsoft Teams for Education provides an online classroom so students and teachers can find new ways to focus on learning. Teams allows you to create a space to collaborate with ease, engage learners, and elevate day-to-day work. Plus, it is *free* for schools and universities.

Microsoft Teams allows teachers and students to

- *Collaborate with ease.* Meet with your students or community members and access persistent chat to ensure everyone stays connected for learning. Current and previous chats are available for access at any time through the chat feature. Microsoft Teams also offers users the ability to seamlessly collaborate through shared files. Files can be viewable or even editable by all team members.

- *Engage learners.* Use the assignments feature, the announcement feature, channels, and partner applications to engage your learners within Teams. Assignments offer an easy way to engage students in learning and assess their knowledge. Announcements offer learners the ability to engage in conversations and polls. Channels encourage the learner to dive deeper into specific information within the channel, the teacher has the ability to customize each channel with engaging content, using various Microsoft partner applications.

- *Elevate day-to-day work.* Access insights for the classroom, use apps and integrations to reduce workloads, and build community, all on a safe and secure platform. Using the "Insights" integration, the teacher is able to see student interaction in detail. Use this information to quickly adjust teaching and student workload, assess the students' social and emotional needs, and encourage students to complete work on time.

Teams Tour

If you are a novice Teams user or a tenured user, we want to give you a quick tour to help you understand the terms we will be using throughout this manual regarding Teams and the layout of this learning platform.

Once you log in to Teams either online at office.com or in any of the Teams applications, you will find yourself on the Teams dashboard. This is where you can create Teams or enter into one of your existing Teams.

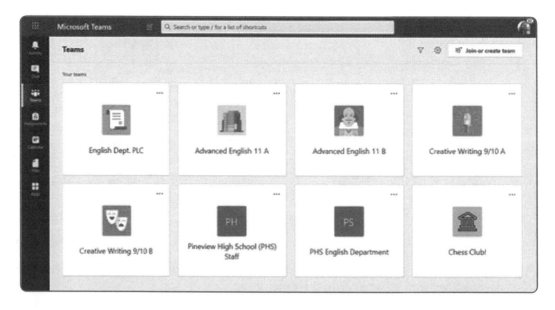

Once you create a Team or select a Team, you will enter the Team. Within this view, you will see three main areas: the "me space," the "we space," and channels.

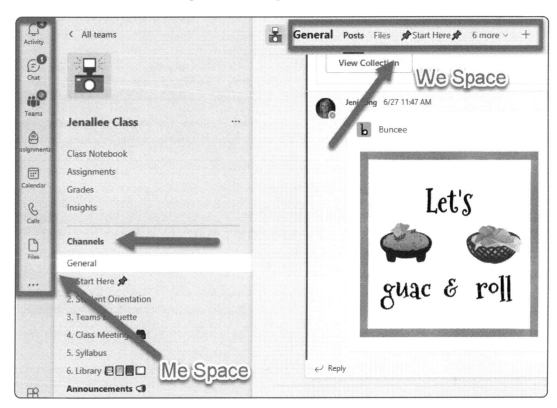

The me space is located on the left-hand side of the screen and runs vertically down the page. We call this the me space because it is all about me. You can view your Teams activity, your chat messages between you and other people within Teams, the Teams you own or are a member of, the assignments of each of your Teams, your Outlook calendar, and your OneDrive files. All of these features are related to you and only shared if you specifically do so.

The we space is the working space on the right-hand side of the page. This is where you will find a bar running across the top of the screen horizontally with key tabs including posts, files, notes, and the plus tab. These features are in a shared space, what we like to call the we space, because everyone has view and (sometimes editable) access to anything in this area. This is where running shared conversations are housed. It feels and looks like social media, and students and educators can post content and interact with content in this space. Files in the we space are stored within Sharepoint. This means that all content is shared amongst the Team members. The files are editable as well. As a teacher in the class, you are able to upload files into a section called "class materials" that allows the files to be viewable, but not editable.

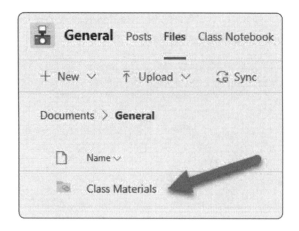

Notes in the we space are built into OneNote. OneNote and Teams work perfectly together to create a cohesive classroom. OneNote is a digital binder, offering your students a Content Library, Collaboration Space, and individual OneNote notebooks. This integration is great for assignments, building a learning portfolio, sharing content with students, and more. The plus tab allows you to add in various partner applications. By adding a top tab with these applications, students can many times remain in Teams and interact within these applications in the we space. Applications include websites, Buncee, Wakelet, Forms, PowerPoint, and more!

You also have the ability to add channels within your Teams. Channels allow you to customize the we space for each channel. As you add channels, you will have posts, files, notes, and top tab options in each channel. This is great for customizing your learning environment. You get to decide how you want to design your team. You can add channels for class information, for questions, for announcements, for units of study, semesters, quarters, etc. Private channels are available as well. This is where you can make channels view-only for specific members of the team. This is great for individual or small group work.

Getting Started

The first step to using Teams is to decide what device you will use. Microsoft Teams is available as a web application and as a desktop application. It can be accessed on all devices, including smartphones, tablets, netbooks, laptops, and computers.

Scan this QR code to see the hardware requirements for Microsoft Teams.

Once you have selected the device you will be using, you will then access Microsoft Teams either through the web at office.com or by opening the Teams application on your device. You can choose to create one of four different types of teams: create a class team, a PLC team, a staff team, or a team for a club or interest group. The table below provides information about each type of team so you can determine which best meets your teaching and learning goals.

- **Class Team:** Select this Team if you are a teacher wanting to host students in a class. It includes assignments, a class OneNote, Teams Meetings, and threaded conversations in posts.
- **PLC Team:** Select this Team to create an educator working group. Great way to collaborate, plan, and share resources. Members of this team share equal read and write permissions. It includes a OneNote, threaded conversations in posts, and shared files.
- **Staff Team:** Select this Team to create a school staff team. Administrators can facilitate staff meetings, shared planning spaces, and individual conversation spaces within the included Staff OneNote. Also included within this Team is Teams Meetings, threaded conversations in posts, and shared files.
- **Other:** Create this type of Team to facilitate clubs and interest groups. Within this Team you can collaborate and plan. This Team shares equal read and write permissions and also has a OneNote.

Scan this QR code for more information about setting up a class, PLC, or staff team.

Now that you've decided which Team type meets your needs, you can learn more about the features of the Team.

Time Out

We are huge fans of the MEC (Microsoft Educator Center). The MEC has a plethora of courses to help educators learn more about Microsoft applications. In taking these courses, you can further your knowledge of these applications, including Microsoft Teams. If you are just getting started with Teams or if you are a pro, check out this course by Matt Miller and Holly Clark: "Making the Most of Teams in the Classroom." Matt Miller, author of *Ditch That Textbook*, and Holly Clark, coauthor of *The Microsoft Infused Classroom*, share their expertise on how to operate Microsoft Teams and use this application in the classroom.

When using Teams to cultivate an equal playing field within your classroom, start by creating and teaching best practices that directly relate to student agency, relevancy, accessibility, assessment, and community. Part 2 will help you design and develop game rules that work best for your team to ensure *all* students have an equitable and accessible learning experience.

"Teams is a wonderful platform that is easy to use and extremely versatile. I love that I am able to house everything I need for class on one platform and not rely on multiple modes of technology that would be confusing to my students. I can also keep everything organized by subject, which is wonderful. I am able to meet, post reminders, create assignments, attach websites that I use, and so much more! The students love how easy it is to navigate from class to class. They love showing their classmates how to add backgrounds and how to use all the different features in meetings. If it were not for Teams, I would have never been able to teach virtually during the pandemic. It has been a lifesaver!"

Katherine Wardlaw (@KatherineWardl1)

PART TWO

Defining the Game Rules: Best Practices

In this section of the coach's manual, we will share best practices we have gleaned from our real-life experiences, including solutions and operational tips and tricks. This is the information we wish we would have had in 2019. We hope this section saves you heartache, frustration, and time as you try to find solutions.

We broke down these best practices into six sections, based on Teams features and school components:

- First Days of School
- Chat
- Posts, Channels, Top Tab
- Meetings
- Assignments
- Accessibility

CHAPTER 5

First Days of School

Teams allows you and your students to communicate, work together, and learn in a common shared space. This shared space is your classroom. As in your physical classroom, you must set and teach the rules, procedures, consequences, and rewards at the beginning of the school year. As Harry Wong notes in *The First Days of School*, "You can accomplish anything with students if you set high expectations for behavior and performance by which you yourself abide." This cannot be neglected—especially in this new digital frontier for students. Educators must directly teach these concepts, practice these concepts, uphold these concepts, and reteach these concepts.

Maybe you are still learning to navigate a digital classroom and don't know where to start. No worries! This section summarizes some things you can do to set the tone for appropriate student etiquette in the Teams environment. Not surprising, building relationship with students is the key, followed closely by expectations, consequences, and rewards. In the physical classroom, teachers always start with these. When introducing Teams to your students either in person, online, or within a hybrid classroom, you must also start with relationships and rules and spend time learning how to operate in this platform.

Building Relationships

As we have already discussed, building relationships with your students from the first day of school is vital to student growth and success! This is true whether you teach in-person or in a hybrid or remote classroom. Making students feel valued, connected, and heard in the classroom should be a teacher's primary goal! When students feel connected, they join in and participate. They are engaged in learning.

Building these relationships takes time, planning, and consistency. Here are ten ideas for building these important relationships and classroom community. The culture in your classroom

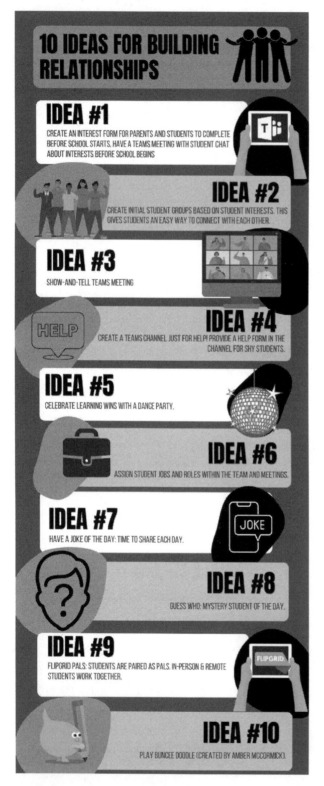

10 IDEAS FOR BUILDING RELATIONSHIPS

IDEA #1
CREATE AN INTEREST FORM FOR PARENTS AND STUDENTS TO COMPLETE BEFORE SCHOOL STARTS. HAVE A TEAMS MEETING WITH STUDENT CHAT ABOUT INTERESTS BEFORE SCHOOL BEGINS

IDEA #2
CREATE INITIAL STUDENT GROUPS BASED ON STUDENT INTERESTS. THIS GIVES STUDENTS AN EASY WAY TO CONNECT WITH EACH OTHER.

IDEA #3
SHOW-AND-TELL TEAMS MEETING

IDEA #4
CREATE A TEAMS CHANNEL JUST FOR HELP! PROVIDE A HELP FORM IN THE CHANNEL FOR SHY STUDENTS.

IDEA #5
CELEBRATE LEARNING WINS WITH A DANCE PARTY.

IDEA #6
ASSIGN STUDENT JOBS AND ROLES WITHIN THE TEAM AND MEETINGS.

IDEA #7
HAVE A JOKE OF THE DAY: TIME TO SHARE EACH DAY.

IDEA #8
GUESS WHO: MYSTERY STUDENT OF THE DAY.

IDEA #9
FLIPGRID PALS: STUDENTS ARE PAIRED AS PALS. IN-PERSON & REMOTE STUDENTS WORK TOGETHER.

IDEA #10
PLAY BUNCEE DOODLE (CREATED BY AMBER MCCORMICK).

is a direct result of your taking time to build a relationship with each student and foster healthy student-to-student relationships. Time spent in these activities during the first days of school sets the culture and community of your classroom for the year.

Expectations

Just as you do in your physical classroom, set your expectations for your Teams classroom! Expectations should be positive and short, and they need to be introduced, explained, and practiced each day. As Harry Wong notes, "The most successful classes are those where the teacher has a clear idea of what is expected from the students, and the students know what the teacher expects from them."

Here are a few keys we have found to be successful in our classrooms. We have three to five rules or expectations; they are short, easy to understand, and positive, and they are explained in depth repeatedly within the first two weeks of school. For example, "Be Respectful" is one of our five rules. However, that can be a very broad expectation. So, we take time to explain it in detail with examples for our students to understand. In person and online, we operate with respect. We speak nicely to people and we respect their property, their person, and their thoughts. We share examples, allow students to share examples, and all agree that this is the way we will function within our classroom. In teaching respect in depth and repeatedly, our students are able to easily transfer this knowledge to the online classroom as well.

What are the expectations in your physical classroom? Take a moment to evaluate them. Do they represent the clear idea of what is expected in your classroom? Do they convey your expectations to the students?

We have created a graphic of expectations for using Teams. Essentially these are the same expectations you would have in your physical classroom. You want students to be respectful of one another, work together, and stay on task.

Scan this QR code to access our expectation graphic. Feel free to use this this or remix it to fit your classroom expectations.

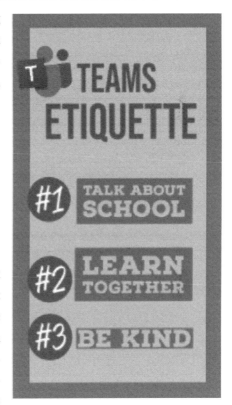

TEAMS ETIQUETTE

#1 TALK ABOUT SCHOOL

#2 LEARN TOGETHER

#3 BE KIND

Consequences

Think carefully about the consequences you want to use. You don't want to employ consequences that halt students from using technology to learn or that remove the technology from their hands. Instead, we think a good place to start is with phone calls to parents, conferences with the student, and a negative impact to citizenship grades. Additionally, we strongly suggest you not punish or offer consequences during the first few weeks of school, especially in remote classrooms. Everyone is trying to learn the rules, how to operate, and how to work together in a shared space. Be slow to delve into consequences. Instead offer students the ability to learn, mess up, and correct their mistakes in a safe learning space.

Rewards

Teams Insights analyzes your team activity. It informs the educator of activity in posts, assignments, OneNote, and channels. It gives the educator a deeper glimpse into the whole child and their approach to learning. You can see whether they are collaborating, communicating, and completing their work. One aspect we love about Insights is called "Praise and Badges." Praise cards can be sent to any student at any time for any reason. What a great way to publicly encourage students and show your approval! Use praise in posts and send these messages to students when needed.

Badges are automatic suggestions from Teams for badges for students in your class. This is a great way for you to see accomplishments easily, and you can even create your own badges! If you want to really make an impact, create a OneNote section for behavior in your OneNote Class notebook. Send badges to each student's individual notebook. Parents can then view their student's behavior information from their OneNote parent links.

Coaches' Corner

Connie Lott, Salleé's mom and principal of a School of Character National Award Recipient, shares this idea for using Teams to create rewards in the classroom:

"Create a schoolwide behavior badge system with Teams and OneNote! I would take this reward system full scale with the entire school, bringing an emphasis to character and the classroom."

Procedures and Routines

Now that we have reviewed the importance of building relationships with your students and discussed establishing expectations, consequences, and rewards for your classroom, we want to share some tips with you to operate within this space. Again, Harry Wong in *The First Days of School* speaks directly to the importance of this saying, "The number one problem in the classroom is not discipline; it is the lack of procedures and routines."

One of the first procedures you want to go over in the first days of school is teaching your students how to use Microsoft Teams to do all the tasks they would do in the physical classroom—how to come to class, behave, ask questions, complete work, and find resources. Whether you are in person, remote, or in a hybrid classroom, teaching your students how to navigate Teams, how to conduct themselves, how to communicate, and how to connect on Teams is imperative to their success. Students need to know these things and more! The first days of school give you the opportunity to teach these concepts to your students and practice them.

How to Come to Class

The first thing you want to teach your students is how to come to class. This can look different depending on how you are conducting school.

- **Remote Classroom**—If you are starting school in a remote setting, we suggest you contact and meet with each parent before the first day of school. During these meetings, share your expectations, consequences, and rewards, as well as how students are to come to class and operate inside of Teams. This ensures the students, parents, and you are all on the same page before school begins.
- **In Person**—If you are starting school in person, we suggest practicing how to log in to Office.com or their SSO, navigate to Teams, and locate their Team. Practice this over and over during the first few weeks of school until all of your students are comfortable logging in and locating their classes.
- **Hybrid Classroom**—In a hybrid classroom, it is imperative your students and you all know how to locate and operate Teams. As with the solely in-person classroom, in a hybrid environment, take time to

IDEAS FOR TEACHING HOW TO COME TO CLASS

Practice makes perfect, but practice can also be monotonous. Be careful not to diminish the awesome learning this platform has to offer by teaching these concepts in a mundane manner. Make it fun!

Create your own newscast in Flipgrid sharing how to log in to Teams

Speed test to see who can log in the fastest

Create your own how-to video on how to log in to Teams

Create an Instagram post with the steps to log in to Teams

Create a OneNote Breakout to practice these skills

Teacher talk show! Teacher interviews students from different classes sharing how they login

Hide fun Games inside of Teams (An Easter Egg) As students get logged in they can go on a hunt for the games

Ask your Principal, Librarian, computer lab teacher, coach, etc. to join in the fun and add content to your class for students to find

teach both your in-person students and your remote students how to locate their Team. As teachers in both physical and virtual spaces simultaneously, it is efficient to access student work, grade, and operate in one space. Teams brings these two worlds together and makes it much more effective to operate out of one space. Teams offers the educator the ability to view student work, grade student work, and give feedback.

The information below gives you additional ideas for teaching students how to come to class.

How to Chat

The chat feature is beneficial to the Teams learning ecosystem, because it allows for learning to be fluid. Students can engage in conversations with the educator or other students, and the learning can continue versus sending emails back and forth, with a delay. A chat thread is created and makes communication much more efficient. The chat feature is an effective way for teachers to contact students. Teachers can use the chat feature to answer questions and further explain concepts taught.

There are three settings for chat in Teams:

- Student to teacher/teacher to student—Students can send chats to teachers but not to other students. Teachers can send chats to students or teachers.
- Teacher to teacher—teachers have chat available and can chat with each other. Student chat is disabled, and students may not chat with teachers or other students. Teachers are not able to contact students through chat.
- Open for all—students and teachers have full use of chat. Both can send chats to students and teachers.

It is important to teach students how to use the chat feature according to your classroom expectations. Teach your expectations directly, and frequently remind students how to interact in this space.

Coaches' Corner

If your administration would like to monitor Teams chats in real time, they can use a proactive approach to safety with a service provider such as Gaggle. Gaggle offers schools a live monitoring service, in which humans monitor the Teams chat and alert administration when concerns arise. In addition, Gaggle monitors Microsoft products and services such as OneDrive, email, attachments, Teams, and more.

Gaggle works with Microsoft Teams. Gaggle is a paid service your district can use, if desired.

Teaching students to use the chat tool with wisdom is vital to the culture, operation, and communication in your classroom. Without guidance and expectations, students are likely to create their own standards, either good or bad. Rather than leaving it up to their discretion, as educators, set the procedures and expectations for how to operate and speak to each other within this digital space for the class. This will ensure that everyone can operate safely and learn effectively within the Team.

Scan this QR code to learn more about Gaggle.

ETIQUETTE

TIPS FOR TEACHING COMMUNICATION ETIQUETTE WITHIN TEAMS

REVIEW HOW WE SPEAK TO EACH OTHER IN PERSON, ONLINE, AND IN PRINT

REMIND STUDENTS TO SPEAK KINDLY, GRACIOUSLY, AND DIRECTLY TO PEOPLE

REMEMBER HUMOR IS NOT SEEN ACROSS PRINT

IT IS IMPORTANT TO KNOW THAT WHAT WE POST ONLINE NEVER GOES AWAY. BE SMART ABOUT WHAT YOU SAY AND DO ONLINE

BE SURE TO TEACH STUDENTS HOW TO USE IMAGES, EMOJIS, AND GIFS ONLINE

How to Locate Teams Meetings

Before hosting a Teams Meeting with your students, instruct their parents and them on how to access and locate the Teams Meetings for your class. The following are some ideas you can use for teaching these skills.

- **Digital Meet the Teacher**—Offer a digital "meet the teacher" meeting during which you can explain how to locate and use Microsoft Teams Meetings. Include the rules and procedures for your class. Take this opportunity to explain to parents how to locate their class Team, where you will be holding meetings, and how to locate their daily work.
- **Pre-recorded Video Directions**—Offer your students pre-recorded video directions on how to access your Teams Meetings.
- **In-Person Training**—Have a class meeting for students and parents to attend in person. Take this opportunity to distribute devices or invite parents and students to bring their technology with them. Allow them time to walk through each step with you, clicking along as you teach them how to access your Teams Meetings.
- **Individual Parent and Student Meetings**—Call each student or parent in Teams, and spend ten minutes with each of them to explain how to locate, access, and join your Teams Meetings.

How to Act in a Teams Meeting

An area of procedures not to be missed is to teach your students and parents how to act in a Teams meeting when the camera and microphone are on in class. Both need to be educated because any parents working remotely may be indirectly involved in the meeting.

When you instruct your students and their parents about Meetings etiquette, use the following as a checklist. Teach your students to do the following:

- Identify a learning area location. This should be a table area—not a bed or main living space—that is free of distractions and is as consistent a location as possible.
- Mute the microphone until they are ready to speak.
- Turn their cameras on and off. Offer them the choice to leave their cameras on or off during meetings. If they want their camera on, instruct them to choose a nondistracting background with no light directly behind them. (As educators, we know the value in students leaving their cameras on for part or all of the instruction time; seeing their

faces and ensuring they are listening and learning is a benefit. But this does not need to be mandatory because it may have a negative effect on some students' learning.)

- Position their face squarely in view.
- Speak directly into the microphone and with gusto.
- Be dressed for the school day.
- Use the controls properly.
- Use the chat feature to ask and answer questions.

Teach parents to do the following:

- Allow students to learn on their own.
- Know when class meetings are, and avoid distracting activities (loud music, TV, video games) in the student learning area during that time.
- Allow their children to communicate in class—with their student voice, *not* with the parents' voice.

Remember this platform is for students, not parents. Ask parents to try not to appear on camera. If they are going to be on camera, ask them to be dressed for an appearance.

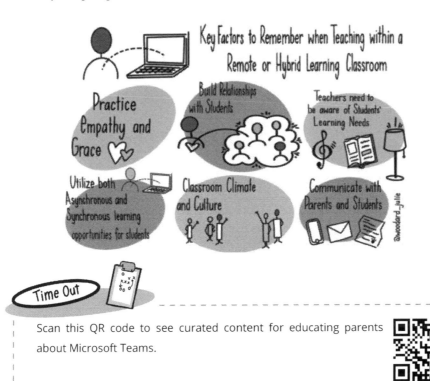

Scan this QR code to see curated content for educating parents about Microsoft Teams.

CHAPTER 6

Chat

Use the Chat tool to maximize your communication and student learning. Teams Chat can be used in three ways:

- Contacting individual students
- Small group chat
- Chat feedback loop

Contacting Individual Students

Chat allows you to contact individual students. When you reach out to students in Chat, they receive a notification and can then respond to your chat message or call you. Regardless of your role in the school, you can easily contact them by simply clicking Chat and then typing the student's name. We believe it is the best communication tool within Teams.

Many students do not want to openly ask for help in a meeting or in a Teams post. Using the chat feature gives students the ability to contact their teacher and ask questions easily. The same is true for teachers. Many teachers do not want to call out a student directly in a call or a post. Chat offers a safe space to communicate with them.

Small Group Chat

Need to foster small group chats? You can do this by creating chat groups. Simply add all of the members you desire to be in the chat and begin a text conversation with the group. The chat remains in each member's feed and allows you to easily reach everyone in one quick chat. You can even personalize the chat group name. Calling everyone in this small group at one time is also easy. Simply open the chat and click the ***call*** button. Everyone in the chat will be instantly called into a face-to-face group meeting via video.

Chat can also be used between teachers and student groups for small group work, reading groups, leveled groups, dyslexia groups, and so forth. Chat is also a great tool for teachers to communicate as a group, hold quick meetings and collaborations, and more.

Feedback Loop

If you need to offer your students individualized feedback, you can create a chat message with them. You can easily send a link to an assignment, post, or announcement in Chat. Keep students in the loop of their progress by answering their questions and offering feedback for their work with chat.

When Chat Is Turned Off

Some districts may choose to disable the Chat feature. When Chat is disabled, teachers will lose the ability to send typed chat messages to students or directly call students. We experienced this in our district and discovered a few work-around tips we shared with our teachers to make communicating with their students more efficient.

- **Create Private Channels.** Create private channels within your team for each student or small group. This gives them a safe place to ask questions and communicate with you without all students seeing the conversation.
- **Raise Your Hand Form.** Create a "raise your hand" form for students to use when they have a question or need help. Students can fill out the form to request you contact them. You can also set up an automatic workflow, called a Microsoft Flow, to trigger specific notifications to email you every time a student completes the form.
- **Create an "I Need Help" Channel.** Channels are dedicated sections within a Team to help keep conversations organized by specific topics, project, time periods, or whatever works for your Team. You can also create a channel for students to use to ask questions. Remind your students everyone in the Team will see the content posted in this channel.

Coaches' Corner

Scan this QR code to see how you can set up a Microsoft Flow for your forms.

 You can also call your students without Chat being turned on. Scan this QR code to see a Jenallee video showing you how.

CHAPTER 7

Channels, Posts, and Top Tab

Within Microsoft Teams, organization can be achieved by using channels, posts, and the top tab. Each of these features allows you to organize your Team within the we space. Channels can be customized to fit the subject, unit, or specific topic being taught. Posts allow you to add content to channels, and top tabs offer the teacher the ability to add partner applications and websites to their channels.

Channels

Channels offers you the ability to organize content for your students. The *benefit* to channels is you get to decide how you want to organize and set up your Team. The *challenge* to channels is you get to decide how you want to organize and set up your Team!

We had to use channels for a while to figure out how and why to use these small but powerful sections. Initially, we encouraged teachers to create channels for units of study or each six-week grading period, or create channels for group work, but, after using this application extensively, we have more "tips and tricks" to share. Teams lets you have up to 200 channels and 30 private channels, including deleted channels, so you can use channels in a number of ways.

- *Organize Channels*—By default, channels are listed alphabetically, but you can use numbers to organize your channels to appear in the exact order you want.
- *Identify Channels*—Using emojis makes it easy to identify your channels. And who doesn't love emojis?! We have seen teachers label each channel with an emoji, and we have seen others label only the channel they are working in.

- *Create a Chat Channel*—Create a channel for students to chat. They want to communicate with each other about everything from what they had for dinner to what time they are getting online to play games tonight. If you don't create a spot for them to chat in your Team, they will chat in your Teams Meetings Chat or in the posts for all sections. So, why not give them a place to hang out and chat?

- *Create a Questions Channel*—We love having a channel where we can include help videos and a place for students to contact us if they have questions. If you don't want students to have to ask for help in a public channel, you can create a Microsoft Help Form and place it in this channel for students to fill out when they need help. Take it a step further and create a Microsoft Flow for the form so you receive an email every time a student fills out the form. This is a great way to allow students to contact you in a non-stigmatizing way.

- *Create a Class Info Channel*—Create a channel for all of your classroom information. You can include expectations, rules, procedures, rewards, syllabi, and so forth. This is a great way to post your rules in your classroom.

- *Create Private Channels*—Create private channels for small group work, collaboration groups, and so forth. Private channels also can be created for special services such as dyslexia, speech, or special education. Add the specialized teacher to your Team as a member and add them to the private channel so they can collaborate.

Coaches' Corner

A channel name can only be used once, so do not delete a channel with a name you want to reuse. Before you delete it, rename the channel to something you would not use, such as "trash" or "delete."

Posts

Posts are the first thing your students see in a Team channel, so it is important to keep them organized and easy to read. Below are a few best practices for keeping this space as useful as possible.

One of our favorite features in the Posts tab is the ability to create an Announcement. When you click on the *A* to open the editing window, you will see the *Announcement option under New conversation.* Creating an announcement allows you to make a post that will stand out. You can even choose who can reply, or post in multiple channels so that everyone will be sure to see the message.

As you begin planning your posts, think about the channel and the purpose of the channel. If the channel is going to be a busy place with questions, feedback, and collaboration, consider the following features and suggestions:

- Use this space for announcements to make sure your content is seen and heard. Consider including illustrations in the banner or custom banner headers to make your post stand out and be easily understood.
- Add video directions to your announcements to engage students and ensure the content is understood. We like using Flipgrid Shorts to create engaging, quick tip videos for students. Flipgrid Shorts offers educators the ability to create stand-alone videos while using the Flipgrid video features, including frames, stickers, backgrounds, and more. You can locate Flipgrid Shorts at the top of your Flipgrid menu once you are signed in to Flipgrid.com.
- Use this busy place to take Form polls quickly to check understanding, find the frequently asked questions, identify student initial knowledge on content, conduct a social/emotional learning (SEL) check, etc.
- Insert links to needed tabs, assignments, and channels. You can hyperlink content in the Team to save clicks and to ensure the students know exactly where to go to access the content in the post.
- Teach students how to use the Reply button rather than always starting a new post.
- Teach students to use academic language and reasoning before posting to a learning channel.

If the channel is only for academic content and you want to be the sole contributor to the posts section, consider the following best practices:

- Manage the channel to allow only owner posts *or* owner posts and student replies. This way you can control the content of posts for this channel.
- Provide a channel that you do not manage solely for students to post chats in. This will encourage the communicative and collaborative aspect of Teams, which is where learning happens.
- Create engaging lessons and content with partner apps such as Adobe Spark, Canva, Nearpod, Buncee, Genially, and more. Send these creations to posts straight from the application. This makes the content easy to share—you use fewer clicks, and students use fewer clicks, because it is the first thing they see when they click on the channel.

- Create a table of contents for each day, linking to associated posts, channels, or assignments. Offer the students a comprehensive spot to find the directions and content they need for their day of learning.

- Use announcements to create daily checklists for your students. At the beginning of the day, post a to-do list for the students to follow. At the end of the day, edit the post to add any further information or recorded Teams Stream videos to make a comprehensive daily checklist. Stream is the application that Microsoft uses to record your Teams Meetings. When you click **Record** in your Teams Meetings, the recording is stored in Stream and can be located, viewed, edited, and downloaded from the Stream app in your Microsoft 365 account at office.com.

- Create a daily update in a Teams post. Recap your day of learning with a quick review, reminders, or other important information.

- Create videos of directions to help students see and understand exactly what you want them to do, and easily insert them into posts. Flipgrid Shorts is our favorite tool for creating these videos. You can record content on your screen for up to ten minutes while using the Flipgrid camera features. Display the work on the screen, and explain, demonstrate, and share step-by-step directions for the work by using the Flipgrid camera features. Adding an image, annotating on the screen, or recording your screen is easy to do with Flipgrid Shorts.

Coaches' Corner

Be sure to check out the background options in Announcements. You can choose from a variety of colors as well as super fun preset backgrounds such as fire-breathing dragons, disco balls, space, school themes, or you can even upload your own image. This is sure to get the attention of every member of your Team. Scan this QR code to see a Jenallee video explaining how to make a custom announcement header with Adobe Spark.

Top Tab

This is one of our favorite parts of Teams! By clicking the "plus" button, often called top tab, you can add learning opportunities, materials, videos, anchor charts, games, interactive websites, and more to your channel. One of the most powerful aspects of the top tab is that you can add partner applications straight into your Team we space. This means students can actively work in the applications without leaving Teams. A few partner applications that we use most often include Buncee, Flipgrid, Wakelet, Adobe, and Forms. Many websites when added will operate within the Teams we space as well.

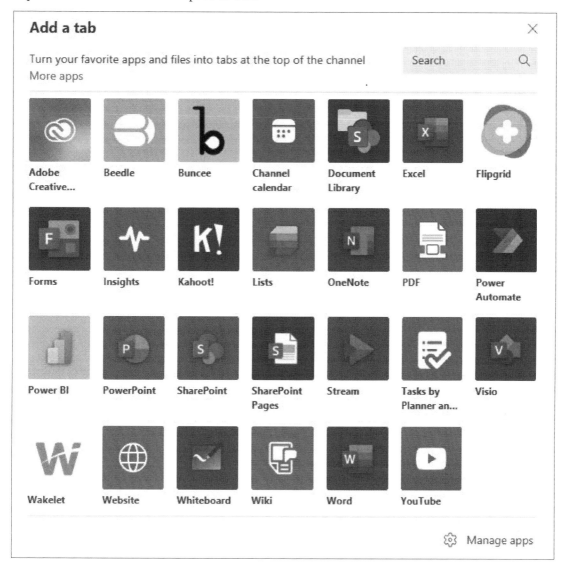

The top tab in each channel offers you the ability to customize the channel to fit what you are teaching during a particular week, unit, quarter, or in a particular HyperDoc. You have the opportunity to design your instruction area with top tabs.

We like this area because many of the items added here are embedded into Teams, which means students can interact with the content without leaving Teams! This is a huge win!

The following are tips you can use when setting up your top tabs:

- Because only a few tabs will show at one time across the top, do not add too many tabs, or it may become too difficult to locate the material.
- Think of this space as your current, active workspace, and use it in this way. You can interchange the content, collaborate, brainstorm, share updates, and more with these helpful add-ins.
- If you are adding an educational product, check to see whether there is a Top Tab app. If you think your resource is a website, check to see whether an app is available for it.
- Activate more apps. Click on *Apps* in the bottom left corner of the me space and add them to more places within your Team!

CHAPTER 8

Meetings

Teams Meetings are helpful for meeting with students, learning remotely, connecting with people outside of the classroom, collaborating on projects, and more! Meetings can be created through channels or by scheduling meetings.

Channel Meetings

We suggest creating meetings with students from within the channel where you want to meet. You can do this by using the Meet button in the top right corner of the we space in your Team. When you select Meet, you will then select Meet Now.

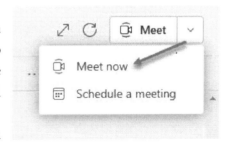

The Channel Meet Now option is good to use, for a number of reasons:

- The meeting automatically posts to the channel you create it in.
- A small purple video camera appears by the name of the channel you are meeting in.
- When the meeting ends, students are not able to restart the meeting.
- Video chat is housed in the channel so you and the students can refer to it again when needed.
- Only two clicks are needed to start the meeting: Meet, then Meet Now.

Scheduled Meetings

You can schedule your Teams meetings in Outlook, within the calendar in Teams, or in the Teams channel. When scheduling your Teams Meetings in Outlook, you can access your address book. When scheduling your Teams Meetings in the Teams calendar, you can schedule the meeting within a specific channel.

Scheduled meetings offer participants a meeting link that can be used every day or for a one-time meeting. This makes scheduled meetings especially helpful when coordinating

- Guest speakers
- Parent meetings
- Conferences with students
- Interviews

Scan this QR code to access directions for setting up a Teams Meeting.

Presenter Permissions

By default, the organizer of the meeting is the presenter for the meeting. They can share their screen and content with the meeting attendees. If you want your students or attendees to present content, you will need to grant them permission in the Meeting Options.

Here's one way to access the Meeting Options:

- Start the meeting.
- Click the three dots in the task bar.
- Select Meeting Options.

Record a Live Lesson in a Teams Meeting

Meetings gives you the option to record your live lessons. This is especially nice for students who were not able to attend your live class. It also offers students a safe and secure network to work in and view content from.

Consider this important information about Teams Meetings recordings:

- Videos are recorded and automatically posted to your Team channel. The videos are also stored in Microsoft Stream. *A1 Microsoft licenses do not have this ability.*
- Microsoft Stream is an application within your Office.com dashboard. Videos can be edited and shared, and Stream channels can be created from Stream. Stream Channels are the perfect solution to a safe and secure playlist for your students. We think they're fantastic!
- If the meetings took place in your Team, by default, only students in your Team will be able to view the recordings. You can change the permissions in Stream to include your entire organization or other Teams you own so others can view them as well.

- All Stream videos are viewable only by your organization.
- All Stream videos can be downloaded to your device.

Daily Recordings

If you teach in a Teams Meeting daily, record these meetings if permitted by your district. *Please consult your district on their recording policies.* The videos are safely stored in Microsoft Stream, easy to share, and safe for your students to view. Recording them also saves you time! By recording live videos, you do not have to record separate lessons or content for asynchronous learning.

Coaches' Corner

Scan this QR code to access a collection of Microsoft Stream resources curated by Principal Product Manager for Microsoft Education, Mike Tholfsen.

Naming Convention

Create a naming convention with each video created. When you start the meeting, click the title and rename it. If you forget, you can always edit the name in Stream.

Share Your Screen

When meeting with students, you may frequently want to share your screen. You may need to share the content on your computer so your students can see and interact with it. Once the meeting is started, you can share your screen. Click on the **Sharrow** (the square with the arrow pointing into it) at the top of your screen. This will allow you to select a screen, window, document, or whiteboard to share.

When you share your screen, these quick tips may be helpful:

- You can share a screen or you can share a window. If you share a window to a specific website, students will only see the website. If you navigate away from the website to another application or site, they will only see the original window you shared. Many times, we will share a window and try to switch to another application and forget that students can only see the original window that was shared. When you share your screen, students will see whatever is on your screen. Then you can seamlessly switch between windows and applications, and students will see whatever is on your screen. As such, we have found it is best to share your *screen* rather than a *window*.
- Students cannot manipulate your computer unless you give them permission.

- Students will see anything you have on your screen. Keep important or private information off the shared screen. Consider putting your computer in **Focus** mode or at least turning off all pop-up notifications (like email and chat).

- You can share an application on your computer for students to manipulate. Click the **Sharrow** and share your screen. Students can then request to control your computer. When the request is granted, you will see your picture and the student's picture on the mouse you are controlling. The student can then manipulate the application on your computer. This function is great for interactive PowerPoints, Buncees, Quizlet sight word cards, etc.

- If you want to share a video with sound, after clicking the **Sharrow**, share your sound by clicking the toggle button above the different windows, which will say "share system audio." If you forget to toggle the button on, simply move your mouse to the top of the screen and select the square with the line through it to share your system audio.

Check out these videos to learn more about how to create and share a Teams Meeting link and new Teams Meeting features for 2021.

Camera Features

You will want to share with your students two main aspects of the camera feature for Meetings. They can select a background, and they can choose their meeting view.

- **Background:** Microsoft Teams offers the ability to add a background, an important skill for students to understand how to use, especially when learning from home. The background allows students' homes to remain unseen, and this protects every child and family.

   To activate a background, students can select one as they enter the meeting, or they can select one by clicking the three dots once they have joined the meeting.

- **Meeting View:** Teams Meetings offers a variety of meeting view options. Viewers can customize their meeting experience with the view of their choice. There are many viewing options for participants using video in a meeting. They can choose Large Gallery Mode or Together Mode, with various background scenes to choose from as well. Each individual can even choose whether to have their camera on or off, choose a specific background or video layout, and even pin or spotlight the speaker.

Interactive Features

Within a Teams Meeting there are a variety of ways that students can interact with the teacher. Students can raise their hand to indicate the need to ask a question. They can also respond to the presentation with emojis. Polls and questions can be asked within the Teams Meeting chat feature as well.

- **Raise Your Hand:** During Teams Meetings, ask students to "raise their hand" if they have a question or if you quickly poll your class. Students can click the hand icon under *Reactions* on the Teams Meeting toolbar. You will see a notification and can see all participants with their hands raised by clicking on the people icon in the toolbar.
- **Emoji Response:** Poll your students with Emoji Responses. This fun addition to Teams Meetings allows students simply to click the "smiley face" icon on the Teams Meeting toolbar and select the emoji of their choice.
- **Chat:** Use the Chat feature for students to ask or answer questions and quickly respond to poll questions you ask. Students can format their chats to add files, emojis, gifs, stickers, and more. Teaching students how to communicate in this academic space is important so that this space can be maximized for learning. One way we maximize learning within Chat is with Formative Assessments from Buncee. We add our Buncee slides to our Teams Meeting. This enables the teacher to add questions for each slide of the presentation. The students can respond in Chat, and their responses are only viewed by the teacher. They are stored in Chat and Buncee for the teacher to review at any time. Be sure to explore app add-ins such as Buncee, Wakelet, and Forms to seamlessly poll and interact within the Teams Meeting Chat.

Coaches' Corner

Scan this QR code for an Emoji Response rubric that you can use with your students.

Coaches' Corner

Check out this playlist with Buncee and Teams integrations. Buncee is an application that encourages creation! Create interactive class-rooms, sorting activities, and presentations within this educational application. This add-in is a great way to maximize the learning pos-sibilities within the Teams platform.

Time Out

Matt Miller has a fantastic resource about how to manage Microsoft Teams Education like a pro! Scan this QR code to check it out!

CHAPTER 9

Assignments

Assignments is a Teams feature that allows for the teacher to create, upload, and build assignments for students within Teams. This allows for the student to complete work within the Teams we space, turn it back in to the teacher, and receive feedback. We are going to share what we have learned about Teams Assignments and what we think is the best way to create, use, and make assignments in Teams.

We will look at the five main Teams Assignments aspects:

- Creation
- OneNote Assignments
- Grades
- Teams Feedback Loop
- Insights

For each aspect, we will share our tips and tricks for using various Teams features to help you use Teams more efficiently and effectively with your students.

Creating Assignments

Tags, naming conventions, and rubrics are helpful features to use when creating assignments.

Tags

Specific tags can be added to assignments using the "add category" feature. This adds quick visual organization and allows you to view and sort all assignments labeled with specific tags.

Coaches' Corner

Check out this Jenallee video to see how tags can help you better organize your assignments.

Naming Convention

Your assignment list is going to get very full as the year progresses. One of the best things you can do is create a naming convention to use throughout the school year. This will help you and your students easily understand and locate assignments.

Check out this Jenallee video to see how to name your assignments.

Rubrics

Check out this Jenallee video to see how to add rubrics to your Teams assignments.

Rubrics allow you to customize your grading criteria. This is good teaching practice and benefits both you and your students. You know what you are assessing and can clearly teach the concepts, and your students understand the expectations for the assignment. Rubrics help you and your students work in purposeful ways to teach and learn together.

In Teams, you can create rubrics from scratch, save and share rubrics, or even upload existing rubrics.

OneNote Assignments in Teams

If you know Jenallee, you know we love OneNote! In fact, we like to say we "bleed purple" for OneNote and Teams. As we began to use Teams more and more, we realized that using OneNote Assignments is the best way to assign work in Teams. These two apps make learning more engaging, organized, efficient, and accessible.

Below are our top five reasons for using OneNote Assignments in Teams:

- A OneNote Notebook "Teacher Only" section allows you to create content for your students in a space that is unseen until you assign the page to your students.
- You can embed content from other edtech applications (Buncee, Wakelet, Genially, Canva, YouTube, and more) directly into your assignments.
- The Learning Tools are excellent!
  - Draw Tool—Students can click on **Draw** and write on PDFs or JPGs, or they can write in the workspace.
  - Immersive Reader—As Mike Tholfsen, principal product manager at Microsoft Education, says, Immersive Reader is "built-in, non-stigmatizing, *free*, and mainstream." As built-in assistive technology within many Microsoft applications, users

can click ***Immersive Reader*** to have anything that has been typed on a page read aloud. Within Immersive Reader, students can customize their experience by using a colored background, changing the font size, zooming in on lines being read, translating a word or document into a different language, and even using a picture dictionary. These functions are built into Teams and OneNote and are customizable by the user.

- Audio—Students and teachers can record their voice in the page. Teachers can read directions or orally administer a test. Students can record their responses or information for the teacher.
- Dictation—Users can click the microphone and speak their thoughts while OneNote dictates the content.

- Students and teachers can insert any type of content, including typed text, links, PDFs, images, and more. When adding a PDF, right click and choose **set as background**. This will assure the document/image will not move around on the page or be deleted by the students. When the PDF is set as a background, the students can type, draw, or dictate right on it.

- As students complete their work throughout the year, OneNote organizes content and creates a Digital Portfolio of the work. You can share a link to give parents the ability to see student work in real time, teacher feedback, and revisions. You also can delete Teams Assignments, and OneNote keeps the student work in OneNote. This helps keep your assignment tab current, while also keeping assignments organized, accessible, and stored in OneNote within Teams.

Check out this Jenallee video to see how to set up your Class OneNote so you can create OneNote assignments in Teams.

Grades

Seeing student submissions and seamlessly grading student work is accomplished with the Grades tab. In this tab, teachers can see each assignment, see student work status, and grade student work.

With this tab, teachers can easily see the due date, title, and tags for each assignment. One of our favorite features is the ability to view student work status at first glance. Grades allows you to quickly see whether students have viewed the assignment or turned it in. You are also able to see whether the assignment has been returned and view the revision status.

Once you view a student's work in the assignment, you can quickly grade other students' work by simply clicking the right or left arrow to make the next student's work appear. You can give feedback, grade, and write notes on the work right in the grading window. It is super-efficient. Plus, we love using the customizable stickers in OneNote when grading work! Microsoft offers a large selection of stickers that you can use to encourage and praise students. Many of these stickers are customizable and allow for the teacher to add personalized notes and feedback for the students.

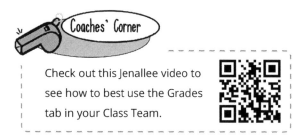

Check out this Jenallee video to see how to best use the Grades tab in your Class Team.

Teams Feedback Loop

The Teams feedback loop is a beneficial feature. While students are working, teachers can leave comments in their ongoing work. As students submit their work, the teacher can leave feedback for students to improve. After improvements have been made by the student, they can resubmit the work, and teachers can view their status with one glance in the Grades tab.

Insights

With the Insights app, you will have access to data from across all of the channels within your class Team. This makes tracking students' activity and progress easier than ever. Through analyzing this data we are able to get a picture of the student as a whole. You can view data about their engagement and work within the Team.

Insights analyzes the following:

- **Digital Engagement**—Student activity within the team, including communication, files, OneNote, meetings, and more

- **Assignments**—Student activity within Assignments, including assignments viewed as well as assignments completed, returned, and on-time submission/late submission details

Get an overview of your Team's digital engagement and the assignments completed. After looking at your class as a whole, you can choose to look at a student's individual data in these areas as well. This information helps a teacher understand their students' communication, collaboration, and work habits. Insights also offers a "spotlight" for educators to use. "Spotlight" shares the important trends found within the student activity in your Team.

Best practice would be to ensure that you have clicked "Get Started with Insights". Insights is now located above channels within your Team. Use this data to help inform your teaching and class management.

Coaches' Corner

If you would like to learn more about Insights and see quotes from other teachers who have used this application, scan this QR code to access a Microsoft article about Insights in Teams.

Time Out

Check out Beedle! Beedle is an application that helps teachers and students in their daily work within Microsoft Teams. To learn more about Beedle, scan the QR code.

CHAPTER 10

Accessibility

As our friend Mike Tholfsen says, "Microsoft learning tools are built-in, mainstream, non-stigmatizing, and free." Why is this so important? As mothers of children with dyslexia, we know having access to content in a non-stigmatizing way is extremely important to our children. They don't want their high school teachers to come to their desks and read content to them; they want access built into their everyday productivity tools. And as parents, we want it for *free*!

Microsoft Learning Tools are built into many Microsoft programs, including Teams, Word, OneNote, and more. See the image below highlighting the various Microsoft Learning Tools' availability.

Microsoft Learning Tools Availability

Learning Tools Flyer for PD: http://aka.ms/LearningToolsFlyer

Microsoft has also partnered with many educational technology applications to offer Immersive Reader within their platforms as well.

Microsoft is continually updating and expanding these features into its products! In addition, they *listen* to their users! Microsoft has developed Microsoft User Voice to enable its users to share their feature requests. Through this website, users can submit feature requests, vote on requests from other users they also would like to see, and view notes from the engineers on the various requests and the statuses of the updates. User Voice really does work; Jenallee has a success story to share! After submitting a User Voice request for Immersive Reader to be added to PowerPoint, users agreed and voted for this feature, and Microsoft delivered. Immersive Reader is now in PowerPoint. Microsoft wants to create a product to empower users to do more. If you want your voice heard, share your thoughts with User Voice.

Scan the QR code to see which apps, sites, and services have currently integrated and launched Microsoft Immersive Reader.

As noted in the preceding chapter, several accessibility tools are built into Microsoft Teams and OneNote:

- Draw Tool
- Immersive Reader
- Audio
- Dictation
- Live Captions for Teams Meetings—Captions will include speaker attribution so participants can see what is being said and also who is saying it.

Scan this QR code to access Microsoft User Voice.

Check out these Microsoft Educator Center courses, interactive guides, and resources to learn more about the Microsoft accessibility tools in Teams.

Scan the QR code to see how easy it is to use Immersive Reader in Microsoft Teams.

Accommodations and Testing

Use OneNote as a Best Practice for Testing and Everyday Accommodations

As you can likely tell by now, we are extremely passionate about creating a learning environment that allows all students equal access to content! Part of this equal access comes through accommodations.

Payton and Hunter each need specific accommodations for them to have a learning experience equivalent to that of their peers. We understand you are busy educators, and it can be difficult to assure your students have the accommodations they need, especially if you have 120 to 150 students. But this does not negate the fact that some of your students need specific accommodations to learn at the same level as their peers. Accommodations are not tools for cheating or just extra work for the teacher. They are imperative to offer each student an equal learning experience.

OneNote Learning Tools are excellent for students with accommodations. These tools are also good for *all* students. All students have access to content in the way they need it, and accessing content is not stigmatizing. It is available on all devices online and in the app! Plus, OneNote is not extra work for the educator, and it is free!

If you have students with oral testing accommodations, consider the following options available with OneNote.

- Students can use Immersive Reader to read the test.
- Teachers can record audio of themselves reading a test for students. (This is our favorite because students can replay the audio as many times as needed for each question without changing the view of the test.)
- Students can use the Edge browser and Immersive Reader to read any website.

OneNote is built into Teams, so teachers can build a test in the teacher section of the Team class OneNote Notebook and then assign it through Teams Assignments to all students or just to the students who need this accommodation.

> "Our teachers are loving OneNote to create assignments in Teams! OneNote works across devices very similarly and has a ton of accessibility tools built in! As a former special education teacher, the accessibility tools in OneNote are a game-changer for students to be successful and confident."
>
> Emily Killen (@EKillen817)

Coaches' Corner

Scan this QR code to access Jenallee's Accessibility Playlist. View videos highlighting Immersive Reader, dictation, inking, audio recording, and more.

Microsoft Edge Benefits

If you haven't taken the leap to make Microsoft Edge your default browser, we recommend you give it a try. The change will be seamless, and all of your current Chrome favorites and extensions will transfer over. You may be surprised at all of the benefits you'll get with Edge. We have listed below a few of the accessibility features in Microsoft Edge:

- **Read Aloud**—Read any website aloud by clicking the three dots in the top right corner, and then "Read Aloud." This makes browsing the web and reading content on any site accessible for all students. Read Aloud also can read many PDFs online.

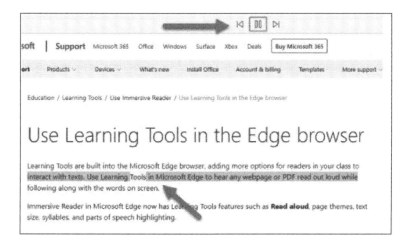

- **Immersive Reader**—Sites with content categorized as "text," usually online articles and blogs, can use Immersive Reader. The Immersive Reader icon will appear in the browser address bar. Click the icon to use Immersive Reader features, including read aloud, backgrounds, picture dictionary, translation, etc.

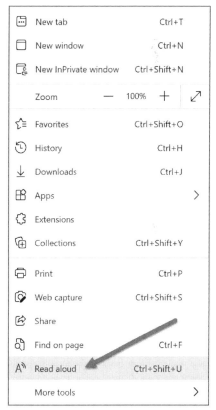

- **QR Maker**—The Edge QR maker offers students quick access to content. By highlighting the address to a site in the Edge browser, the QR code maker icon will appear. Simply click the icon, and a QR code for the site will be created. Share or display this code for students to easily scan to access the site. This eliminates the time it takes an educator to create shortened URLs or hyperlinks, and it makes accessing sites available for all students because of not needing to type the site address into a browser.

- **Digital Inking**—Open PDFs in Edge to ink on the document. Digital inking is built into the Edge PDF viewer. This is a great way to write online versus typing on documents. In addition, all inking on PDFs can be saved as documents. This makes it easy to complete work digitally. This is great for students who do not have access to printers but have a touch-screen device.

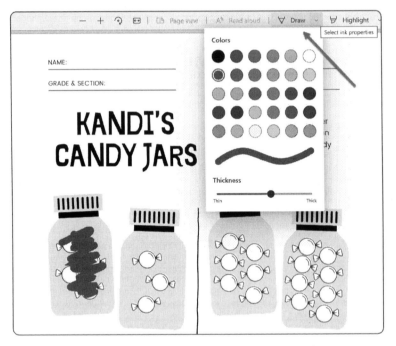

Encourage your students to set Edge as their default browser to have access to Read Aloud, Immersive Reader, and Inking.

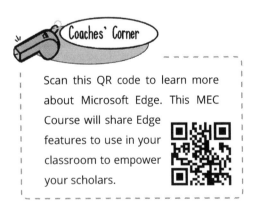

Coaches' Corner

Scan this QR code to learn more about Microsoft Edge. This MEC Course will share Edge features to use in your classroom to empower your scholars.

Time Out

Scan this QR code to access Jenallee's TikTok playlist of Microsoft Edge tips.

CHAPTER 11

Interactive Teaching

When teaching in Teams, teachers and students have the ability to interact with each other in real time by using whiteboard applications. Within these applications, students and teachers can simultaneously interact on the whiteboards, while not being in the same location together. There are many different ways educators can use these applications within the classroom, for example, move manipulatives, annotate passages, sort objects, etc. We have used three whiteboard applications to work in real time with our students during remote, hybrid, and in-person teaching. These whiteboards came in very handy during remote and hybrid learning, because our students at home could sort objects or build words on the whiteboard, while the teacher could see and communicate with the student as they were working.

We have found three whiteboards that work well within the Microsoft Teams Ecosystem:

- Microsoft Whiteboard
- Whiteboard.chat
- OneNote

Microsoft Whiteboard

Microsoft Whiteboard is a free-form, infinite digital canvas where you and your students can share content, and ideas magically come together. "Whiteboard integration in Microsoft Teams Meetings is powered by the Whiteboard web app, which lets Teams Meeting participants draw, sketch, and write together on a shared digital canvas." ("Manage the Whiteboard in Microsoft Teams," 2021)

Using Microsoft Whiteboard in a Teams Meeting is beneficial for the following reasons:

- Whiteboard is built into the "sharrow" as an app to share.
- As you share the app, you can decide whether the whiteboard is to be collaborative.

- You can add manipulative content (images, pdfs, documents) to the whiteboard, and students can write, draw, and move added content around, etc. This feature is helpful for building words, solving math problems, or creating mind maps together.
- Whiteboards are saved in the Microsoft Whiteboard cloud and accessible through the Windows 10 application.
- You can export images and content from Whiteboard.
- Whiteboard has an infinite canvas. Once you are finished with one area of the whiteboard, you can move the canvas to another section and continue to work. It will continue on and move infinitely.
- Immersive Reader is built into Whiteboard and will read typed text within the Whiteboard.
- You can also add Microsoft Whiteboard as a Top Tab in Teams.

Whiteboard.chat

Whiteboard.chat is a web-based whiteboard designed for teachers. Manipulatives, tools, and classroom-focused features are built into Whiteboard.chat. Because Whiteboard.chat is a web-based application, it works seamlessly with any LMS platform, and it allows you to share your boards with students via a QR code, link, or code.

With Whiteboard.chat, you have the option to ***start teaching*** or ***start collaborating***. ***Start teaching*** generates a copy of your whiteboard for each individual student who joins your board. You can easily see each student's board, interact with each student's board, and chat with students. ***Start collaborating*** generates one whiteboard for the teacher and students. All the students who join the board can collaborate on the same board at the same time.

Whiteboard.chat allows you to:

- Easily share with students via QR code, link, or code (no login required for students). You can share the board within Teams as a Post, Assignment, or Top Tab.
- Whiteboards that you create can be shared as templates with students. The content will be copied to each student's individual board, offering them the ability to individually complete the work on the template.
- Because students have their own individual boards from the template, the educator is able to view all students' work in real time. Educators can click into each board and interact with the student in real time.
- When building templates, educators can use the built-in tools—manipulatives, shapes, text, dice, tile factory—or embed content such as websites and YouTube videos.

- Accessibility tools are built in. Students and educators have the opportunity to record audio or video, and Immersive Reader is built into Whiteboard.chat!
- You can also embed Whiteboard.chat in OneNote. Copy the link to the Whiteboard and paste it into OneNote or OneNote Class Notebook. The Whiteboard will automatically embed and become editable within OneNote.

OneNote as a Whiteboard

As mentioned earlier, we are huge OneNote fans. OneNote and Teams work perfectly together to create a cohesive classroom. OneNote is a digital binder offering your classroom a Content Library, Collaboration Space, and Individual Notebooks.

OneNote can be used as a whiteboard in a Teams Meeting, which is beneficial because you can direct teach using a OneNote page in your OneNote Class Notebook Content Library.

Share your screen in a Teams Meeting so all of your students can view your work. After the meeting, distribute this page to your students' notebooks for them to refer to as they complete independent work, or simply teach students how to locate your content in the Content Library of the Teams Class OneNote Notebook.

Using OneNote in a Teams Meeting as a whiteboard is beneficial for several reasons:

- OneNote Class Notebooks are built into Teams
- Anchor charts, notes, and examples for students to refer to in the Content Library can be created
- Teachers or students can
  - Use the draw tools to ink onto the OneNote page
  - Use the draw tools to ink onto a PDF or JPG
  - Use the Math tools built into OneNote
  - Generate math practice quizzes using the Math tools in OneNote
  - Distribute the page to the students' notebooks when needed

Attach the OneNote "whiteboard" page from the Teams Meeting to an assignment in Teams by including the link to the page. This is a great way for students to easily reference notes while completing assignments.

Coaches` Corner

Canva.com has whiteboard templates you can insert into your online white-board to help facilitate collaboration. These templates work great in Microsoft Whiteboard, Whiteboard.chat, and OneNote.

Time Out

Scan this QR code to see additional Whiteboard lessons and app updates.

PART THREE

Learn the Plays

Now we get into the fun part of the book—the actual *playbook*! As we mentioned before, Teams is much more than a Learning Management System; it truly is a learning *ecosystem*. Microsoft has partnered with many other applications to make Teams an ecosystem of inclusive, interactive, and engaging learning.

We have included in this section some of our favorite partner applications with Teams:

This list is not comprehensive, but these are our go-to applications to use with Microsoft Teams. Please remember, you don't have to use Teams exclusively to use these tools. They work with Google Classroom or other LMSs as well.

Coaches' Corner

If you feel overwhelmed in this section, simply select one app and own it. Don't feel like you have to learn everything all at once. Less is best!

Your Teams Playbook

This section is full of "plays" (lesson ideas) you can apply and use in your classroom. The plays include templates, resources, and tutorials to help you implement these activities with your students. Additionally, a "Scouting Profile" at the beginning of each application gives you a quick glance at the key features of the application. Each profile includes the following key information:

ACCESSIBILITY: accessibility features the application offers

👪 **GRADES:** appropriate user age for best benefit from the application

PRICE: cost of the application (Most applications mentioned are free ⭐, and some offer limited free accounts with upgrade possibilities ⬆️.)

🏆 **TOP FEATURES:** quick list of the most popular features of the application

💬 **GET CONNECTED:** resources to learn more and get connected with the application's community

💡 **MEC COURSE:** Microsoft Educator Center courses to learn more about how to use the various applications

📝 **JENALLEE BLOG:** our reflections and ideas about using the application in the classroom

For the MEC Courses, we suggest you create an account with your school or personal Microsoft account to receive badges, certificates, and points, which will be beneficial in building your Microsoft Innovator Educator portfolio. Other key information is included in the High Five sections, where QR codes offer you quick links to videos, templates, resources, and more.

Finally, we believe in the power of community and love to hear from other teachers and EdTech coaches who are using these tools. Check out the quotes from our friends around the world to hear their stories and why they feel strongly about each application.

OneNote

Overview of OneNote

OneNote is the ultimate digital notebook—a place to keep everything organized—a 21st-century version of the Trapper Keeper notebook we had in the sixth grade. Anyone else remember those? Oh, the memories of our beloved Trapper Keepers that kept all of our papers nice and neat and in one place! Well, Jeni's at least. Even a Trapper Keeper could not help me (Salleé) keep up with anything! Where was OneNote when I was in middle school?

OneNote allows you to keep content organized and to do so much more! OneNote has sections and pages like a notebook, and it also has the ability to embed content from all over the internet, including videos, images, applications, PDFs, emails, etc. You can also ink, dictate, add audio recordings, type, use Immersive Reader, and more!

Say goodbye to Trapper Keeper and hello to OneNote!

 Coaches' Corner

Our friend Chris Gerrard, Digital Learning Consultant and fellow MIE Expert from Scotland, shares excellent information in his Wakelet blog post about embedding content in OneNote.

"

"Over the past 3 years, our district has experienced a lot of virtual learning. Teams and OneNote have been a vital part in keeping our students in school. In 2018, Hurricane Florence devastated our district and our students were out of school for 3 months. Microsoft Teams and OneNote were invaluable tools to keep our students learning. Fast forward to 2020, our schools went to virtual learning in March due to the COVID-19 pandemic, and Onslow County Schools only missed 1 instructional day since the district already used Teams and OneNote as our LMS. Now, we are using Teams as our main communication tool for hybrid learning. Our students attend class in person twice a week and call in to class the other three days. All assignments are completed through Teams and OneNote class notebooks. Teachers use the OneNote for journaling, breakouts, online notes, and group collaboration with students at home and at school. Many teachers use Teams and OneNote as a virtual binder and agenda to help with student organization."

Sachelle Dorencamp (@SachelleD)

OneNote Play #1: Learn the Tools

PLAY DETAILS

DATA PORTFOLIOS

GRADES:
K–12

APPS:
Teams
OneNote

TEAMS INTEGRATION:
Assignment
Channel Top Tab

Lesson Idea

When you teach with OneNote assignments in Teams, we suggest your first assignment consist of fun activities to help students learn how to use the available tools. This lesson idea comes from Meagan Heflin, a teacher in EMS ISD, who helped us develop and implement this activity. She invited her students to use the following tools initially, simply to answer specific questions regarding the specific tools being used in OneNote. These tools include:

- Dictation
- Audio Recording
- Typing
- Draw Tool
- Immersive Reader
- Stickers

#Jenallee

Scan this QR code to see a Jenallee tutorial video for how to use this in the classroom.

The questions were simple and asked students to use these tools to answer the question. For example:

- What is your favorite hobby?
- When is your birthday? Tell me by using the dictate tool to type the date.
- Draw your favorite animal, using the Draw tab in OneNote.
- Use Immersive Reader to read our class rules.

This lesson allowed students to use each of the accessibility tools within OneNote and Teams and allowed the teacher to assess immediately and identify the students who did not know how to use these tools. She then met with those students individually to teach them the skills.

Doing this exercise as you begin to use OneNote with your students is important because it allows them to get comfortable using the app and equips them to use these tools throughout the year and become productive members of your class as you assign work within Teams.

OneNote Play #2: OneNote HyperDoc

PLAY DETAILS
DATA PORTFOLIOS

GRADES:
3–12

APPS:
Teams
OneNote

TEAMS INTEGRATION:
Assignment
Teams Top Tab
Teams OneNote Class notebook

Lesson Idea

As we mentioned earlier in the book, we love using HyperDocs, and they help us go through the entire learning cycle with our students while teaching, assessing, and challenging their thinking. We suggest creating your HyperDocs in your Teams OneNote Notebooks, for three primary reasons:

#Jenallee

Scan this QR code to see a OneNote HyperDocexample.

- Many educational applications and websites embed into OneNote. This is beneficial because, although it is not a document with links to external sites, external content is embedded into your OneNote notebook in Teams!
- When you create your HyperDocs in OneNote assignments in Teams and assign them to your students, they each get their own copy and can interact with the embedded content and even add their own content.
- The accessibility tools are fantastic! All students can access content in OneNote through the built-in accessibility tools such as Immersive Reader, Dictation, Replay, voice recording, etc.

OneNote Play #3: Digital Worksheets and Verbal Justification

PLAY DETAILS
DATA PORTFOLIOS

GRADES:
3–12

APPS:
Teams
OneNote

TEAMS INTEGRATION:
Assignment
Teams OneNote Class notebook

Lesson Idea

One of the most important skills for students is to be able to demonstrate their knowledge of concepts, and one of the most basic needs of teachers is to be able to quickly assess knowledge. Students can demonstrate their knowledge of the content and justify their thinking by using the voice recorder in OneNote. Using a PDF in OneNote as a digital worksheet allows teachers to quickly assess and take the learning up to another level! You can ask students to complete a digital worksheet and add verbal justification to their answers. Students can demonstrate their knowledge with a worksheet by inking, dictating, or typing in content. They are also able to process their answers and verbally justify their thoughts with the audio feature in OneNote.

Teachers can easily assess written work while also understanding the students' thoughts behind their demonstrations of learning! Not only can the teacher see what the students are thinking, they can quickly and easily offer feedback and return the work to students without lugging home a bucket of papers! Teachers also can offer engaging and relevant feedback by using audio feedback, stickers, video (OneNote2016 video player or Flipgrid Shorts embedded), and text.

Empowering Learners' Voice

We have identified these five steps to help empower the voices of learners:

#Jenallee

Scan this QR code to view a video tutorial for how to create a OneNote digital worksheet assignment.

1. Teacher inserts a PDF or image into OneNote and sets it as a background.
2. Teacher assigns the OneNote page to students through Teams Assignments.
3. Students access the PDF through assignments.
4. Students show their work by inking, typing, or dictating answers onto the document.
5. Students justify their work by recording audio and explaining their thoughts.

"

"OneNote class notebook (or jotter as we say in Scotland) is something that has transformed my classroom. I use it as my whiteboard in class (for board notes), as I can insert our PowerPoint as a printout and annotate over it as well as insert the original file. Students can access the notes and all the scribbles at any time. I distribute pages to my students quickly, even during a lesson, and they follow along with what I show on the board. We have linked it with Teams, so all our assignments are OneNote pages...and don't get me started on embedding! I insert a link to a YouTube video and kids can access that and a Forms quiz link right there on the page. To say I love it is an understatement. It has revolutionized teaching and learning in my class and in schools across Scotland. There is no other tool like it!"

Sarah Clark (@Sfm36)

"

OneNote Play #4: Breakouts in OneNote

Lesson Idea

Bring problem-solving to your unit of study by incorporating a OneNote Breakout. Breakouts allow students to work together in groups to solve problems associated with their unit of study. Through solving the problems, they receive a code to unlock the next section. Sound familiar? This is the educational version of a digital escape room! Breakouts are fun and engaging—a great way to introduce content, explore content, or review learned content.

PLAY DETAILS
DATA PORTFOLIOS

GRADES:
3–12

APPS:
Teams
OneNote
Word

TEAMS INTEGRATION:
Assignment

Integrate these games into your lessons in Teams in two easy steps:

- Create your OneNote Breakout or use the templates provided below.
- Share the breakout with your students in Teams.
    - You can share the OneNote link with your students.
    - You can add the pages to your Class OneNote Notebook in the Teacher section and then distribute or assign the section to your class.

Here's how it works:

1. Students complete the tasks and answer the questions for each section of the OneNote.
2. With each right answer and new challenge, another section will unlock.
3. The first group of students to complete the challenges wins the breakout activity.

#Jenallee

Scan this QR code to learn more about OneNote breakouts and receive editable templates.

— 66 —

"The ability to password protect sections in OneNote makes it ideal for creating digital breakouts. I like how easily things embed in OneNote, and how easily it can be shared with others. Furthermore, ease of access across all platforms makes OneNote my go-to program for digital breakout creation."

Bob Eikenberry (@BobEikenberry)

99 —

OneNote Play #5:
Data Portfolios in OneNote

PLAY DETAILS

DATA PORTFOLIOS

GRADES:
1–12

APPS:
Teams
OneNote
Word

TEAMS INTEGRATION:
Assignment

Lesson Idea

Say goodbye to giant binders, paperwork samples, and printed benchmark data. Say hello to the new *digital* student data binder in OneNote. Use the OneNote Class Notebook to collect data and work samples, and track trends and needs through organizing and analyzing the content online. Your students and parents also can be involved in setting student goals, tracking progress, and continually updating their goals—all key to meeting goals!

With one click you can distribute data collection sheets and smart goal sheets to your students' OneNote Class Notebook sections. You and your students can frequently visit this section to update progress and goals. Want to get your parents involved? Set up parent links and share with them. They can see every OneNote assignment their child completes and see their child's progress and goals throughout the entire year. We love involving students and parents in this process so they can both see and understand the importance of every small progress made!

#Jenallee

Scan this QR code to view a video with step-by-step directions for setting up your OneNote data binder.

OneNote Play #6: Math Practice

PLAY DETAILS

DATA PORTFOLIOS

GRADES:
4–12

APPS:
Teams
OneNote
Forms

TEAMS INTEGRATION:
Assignment
OneNote Class notebook

Lesson Idea

Students can practice math skills by checking their work with OneNote Math Tools this way:

- Ink or type a math problem into their OneNote Class Notebook.
- Check their work using Math Tools.
- Generate a Forms practice quiz.

Math Tools solve the math problem and show students step-by-step directions for solving the problem. Students can check their work to ensure that they understand the steps.

If students need further practice, no problem! After they see the steps to solve the problem, students can generate a Forms practice quiz that will embed into OneNote. The Form includes problems similar to the problem they have written into OneNote! You the teacher also can see the quiz and Form results in the OneNote student section.

Scan this QR code to see how our friend Adam Grocott, a math teacher from Jersey, United Kingdom, uses OneNote Math Tools in his classroom!

Scan this QR code to see additional OneNote lessons.

"For me and my students, the OneNote Class Notebook is the most impactful learning tool to come about in my time in education, and it all revolves around providing timely student feedback. Especially in Math, students can significantly increase their understanding of the subject when they receive consistent, frequent feedback to correct their mistakes and make sure they're on the right track. The time I save not having to collect papers in class or wait a couple of days for students to turn in work allows me to focus on leaving thoughtful comments for my students to help them learn the material and close that learning gap that we all know needs to happen to get students to truly love and appreciate the learning process."

Scott Bricker (@BrickerCoaching)

Forms

Overview of Forms

Microsoft Forms is a survey and quiz tool that allows you to quickly retrieve information through digitally asking multiple-choice questions, short and long text questions, scale options, and more. You can quickly assess content learned with the quiz option. Forms offers teachers the ability to mark correct answers, and it will auto-grade quiz submissions.

"Teams allows you to quickly create a new Microsoft Form directly within Teams itself, or you can easily add an existing Form. When the Form is set to collaborate, you and your teammates can edit it together."

Jason Ferrell (@lumberaggie)

Coaches' Corner

When creating a form for student submissions, be sure to create in Forms, not Teams. Teams is collaborative; if you create in Teams from the Forms top tab, the team will own it, and students will be able to edit the form.

Forms Play #1: SEL Check

Lesson Idea

Encouraging healthy mental habits for your students is important. You can create a form that asks specific questions to identify social-emotional needs and use it to check on your students. Students can use forms to take a self-evaluation that informs the teacher of their social and emotional status.

By using Forms branching, you can customize students' evaluations to offer ideas about how they can remain healthy. For example, a question that asks, "How are you feeling today?" could have answer choices (a) *happy*, (b) *sad*, (c) *tired*, and (d) *stressed*. For each answer, the form branches to specific content for that answer. If students select (c) *tired*, the form branches to a section with a yoga video to help them re-energize. If students click (d) *stressed*, the form can branch to a section with a Headspace meditation video. Branching allows you to customize an SEL form for your students.

Place this form where it is accessible by your students in your team. One significant feature of Forms is that you can see the names and responses, but your students cannot see each other's responses.

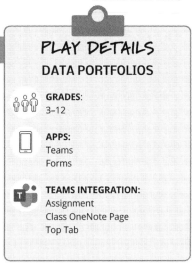

PLAY DETAILS

DATA PORTFOLIOS

GRADES:
3–12

APPS:
Teams
Forms

TEAMS INTEGRATION:
Assignment
Class OneNote Page
Top Tab

Coaches' Corner

Want to do this with math, science, or any subject questions? You can! Simply create the form with the questions and branch each answer to a video, explanation, etc.

#Jenallee

Scan the QR code for an editable template you can use with your students. Also check out the video example for directions on creating the form, setting up a Flow, and posting it to your Team.

Forms Play #2: Help Form

PLAY DETAILS

DATA PORTFOLIOS

GRADES:
3–12

APPS:
Teams
Forms

TEAMS INTEGRATION:
Assignment
Class OneNote Page
Top Tab

Lesson Idea

Students sometimes find it difficult to ask for help in person—or even online. They may feel too intimidated to ask questions in a public post or during a Teams call. With Forms you can offer them a safe way to "raise their hand."

1. Create a Form in Office.com and add it to a Top Tab in your Team.
2. Students fill out the form to ask for help.
3. You can receive an email or text every time a student needs help by setting up a Microsoft Power Automate.

Use Power Automate to seamlessly automate many daily activities. You can eliminate many "clicks" you make in your daily activities. Instead of having to check Form results in Office.com, create a Flow and send the results automatically to your email!

#Jenallee

Scan this QR code for access to a Form template and a video tutorial related to this idea.

Forms Play #3: Book Request Form

Scan this QR code for access to a Form template of this idea.

Lesson Idea

To ensure all students have available content to read that is of interest to them, use Forms to create a book request form for your classroom library.

1. Create a book request form that lists "top reads" for students to choose from.
2. Add the form to Teams as a Top Tab
3. Set up a Flow to alert you when a student wants specific reading materials.

PLAY DETAILS
DATA PORTFOLIOS

GRADES:
3–12

APPS:
Teams
Forms

TEAMS INTEGRATION:
Assignment
Channel
Top Tab

Forms Play #4: Assessment

Lesson Idea

Beginning of Lesson: Create forms to assess students' knowledge at the beginning of your unit. Try to also gauge content you can use to connect to previous knowledge. Insert the form at the beginning of your HyperDoc, embed it in a OneNote Assignment, or insert as a Top Tab in Teams.

During Lesson: During the lesson cycle, use Forms to quickly assess students' knowledge gained and gauge their level of understanding. Use this data to help guide and change your teaching approach as you continue teaching through the lesson. Use this as an exit ticket or quick formative assessment. You also can download an Excel document with form results to identify trends as you plan your direct teaching portion of the lesson.

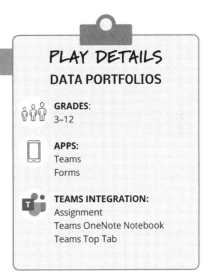

PLAY DETAILS
DATA PORTFOLIOS

GRADES:
3–12

APPS:
Teams
Forms

TEAMS INTEGRATION:
Assignment
Teams OneNote Notebook
Teams Top Tab

Conclusion of Lesson: After the lesson, use Forms to create a summative assessment to discover students' understanding of a concept. Because it auto-grades content, Forms makes it easy to see results! Use a Forms quiz, mark the correct answers, add points, and quickly see your students' test grades populate as they complete the Forms quiz.

#Jenallee

Scan this QR code to see how to create a Forms quiz and share it to Teams to auto-grade your assessment.

Forms Play #5: Polls in Teams

Lesson Idea

Quickly poll students within your Team by using forms in a Teams post! You can use this for a quick formative assessment, to check on the social and emotional status of the group, or even to engage and communicate with your students with fun daily community-building activities.

Follow these steps to add a poll to any Forms post:

1. Click the three dots in the top right corner of the post.
2. Click on *More Actions*.
3. Click on *Create New Forms Poll*.
4. Create the poll questions.
5. View the anonymous answers, which will automatically appear within the post.
6. Instantly create your form.
7. Send to the chat.
8. The poll will appear in the chat area for the students to complete.

PLAY DETAILS

DATA PORTFOLIOS

GRADES:
3–12

APPS:
Teams
Forms

TEAMS INTEGRATION:
Assignment
Channel
Top Tab

#Jenallee

Scan this QR code to see how to add a Forms Poll to a Teams Meeting!

Genially

SCOUTING PROFILE

ACCESSIBILITY

GRADES   **PRICE**

TOP FEATURES

- Create stunning and engaging graphics, games, and presentations.
- Embed into OneNote and Teams top tab.
- Easily share Genially creations.
- Add collaborators.
- Numerous templates.

GET CONNECTED

JENALLEE BLOG

MEC RESOURCES

Overview of Genially

Genially is an edtech platform that allow users to create digital content, from games to presentations to interactive images. With premade templates, teachers simply need to enter their content and let Genially do the rest. All transitions and animations are built in. If you like to create your own from scratch, you can do that too in Genially. You also can share your creations with fellow teachers and collaborate with them on Genially creations. In this digital age of information and digital content overload, Genially helps you find other creations for inspiration and bring engaging visual content to your students.

Our favorite part is that Genially embeds into OneNote! You can embed Genially into OneNote or add it as a top tab in Teams. This makes learning fun, engaging, and easy for teachers.

"Genially is a game-changing tool that allows educators to bring interactivity to any of their creations. By using Genially, you can create interactive presentations, interactive infographics, or online games for gamification. The only limit of Genially is your imagination."

eTwinz (Mario & Alberto Herraez @eTwinzEDU)

Genially Play #1: Gaming

Lesson Idea

Bring gamification to your classroom content with Genially. Genially has many game templates for you to customize for your classroom. Simply click on the questions and answer choices and change them to fit your needs. Creating games for the classroom has never been easier. Not only is it easy, but Genially creations are also visually appealing. Genially also embeds seamlessly into OneNote! Additionally, Genially games embed and bring gamification into your Teams assignments.

PLAY DETAILS
DATA PORTFOLIOS

GRADES:
3–12

APPS:
Teams
Genially
OneNote

TEAMS INTEGRATION:
Assignment
Class OneNote Notebook
Teams Top Tab

For example, we used Genially's "Spin the Wheel" template to create a quick assessment for our students, simply entering our content into the Genially template. After creating the game, we copied and pasted the link to the game into a OneNote page in our "teacher only" section of our Teams OneNote Class Notebook, and the game embedded right into the page.

But we wanted to take a step further, so we embedded our anchor chart as well, helping students recall and practice using their strategies to solve the problems. We also wanted to see what our students were thinking as they completed their work, so we added an answer sheet under the game for the students to complete. With this we were able to see their thinking and justification for their answers. Our students also had access to the Draw tool, Immersive Reader, dictation, and audio recording.

Students can play the game without a login and, because Genially does not store student data, their work is not accessible by others.

Scan this QR code for directions to create, embed, and share your Genially OneNote games.

 Coaches' Corner

Anytime you can use edtech for students to demonstrate their knowledge through written or verbal justification, you offer them the opportunity to truly understand their thinking. In turn, you get a glimpse of their thinking process and can adjust your teaching methods accordingly.

Genially Play #2: Choice Board

PLAY DETAILS
DATA PORTFOLIOS

GRADES:
3–12

APPS:
Teams
Genially
OneNote

TEAMS INTEGRATION:
Assignment
Teams OneNote Notebook

Lesson Idea

One of our favorite ways to use Genially is to create choice boards, which give students choice in which activities to pursue, in the order they choose. Genially has a template created specifically for choice boards, or you can create your own with any of the templates you want to use. We tend to select interactive images or horizontal infographics when creating choice boards. Creating choice boards using Genially is easy; the content is engaging, with games or interactive images; and the content embeds into OneNote!

We like to embed the choice board into our OneNote HyperDocs. Using a HyperDoc for instruction gives students the opportunity to explore content.

In our Jenallee interview with our friend Lisa Highfill, she said to offer students a way to reflect on their exploration. This is a vital part of the lesson cycle because you want to ensure students are exploring content with a driving question in mind, and you need to see what they learned from the content. By understanding what they are thinking, you can form your direct teaching moment to steer the students in the right direction, answer their questions, and make sure they truly understand the concepts.

When using Genially for choice board creation, we suggest you do the following:

1. Select a template for the choice board: the Genially choice board template, an interactive image template, or a horizontal infographic template.
2. Enter the content for students to explore.
3. Link one of the options to a formative assessment option or add a place for formative assessment within the OneNote page.

Easily link Flipgrid, OneNote, Wakelet, and Teams Posts—great ways to see student thinking for formative assessments—to the Genially for students to finish their exploration with a reflection. Embed these choice boards in your class OneNote notebooks as a Teams assignment, top tab, or post.

Genially Play #3: Voice Recording

Lesson Idea

Incorporating audio content is an important part of making learning accessible for all. Genially has audio recording built into its platform, and teachers can use this feature in different ways within their Genially creations. They can

- Record directions
- Read questions
- Read content
- Give an explanation of content
- Offer strategies for completing the work
- Remind students of important tasks
- Use it for younger children who cannot read the content

Insert audio recordings into any of your Genially creations. You can add these as Teams assignments, top tabs, or Teams Posts, or you can even embed them into your Teams OneNote notebooks.

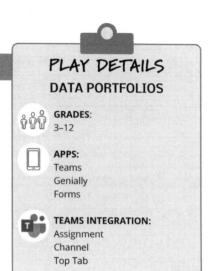

PLAY DETAILS

DATA PORTFOLIOS

GRADES:
3–12

APPS:
Teams
Genially
Forms

TEAMS INTEGRATION:
Assignment
Channel
Top Tab

#Jenallee

Scan this QR code to see how to add audio recordings in Genially.

Genially Play #4: Weekly Calendars

Offer your students an interactive view of their weekly work with Genially and Teams by creating a weekly Genially calendar with links to Teams assignments, posts, and content for students to access each day. Make it even easier by posting your Genially calendar as a Teams top tab or in a Teams announcement. Visually engaging students with a Genially calendar makes it easy for students to look at and remember the work they need to complete.

Follow the steps below so students will know where to locate the fun calendar within Teams.

PLAY DETAILS

DATA PORTFOLIOS

GRADES:
K–12

APPS:
Teams
Genially
OneNote

TEAMS INTEGRATION:
Assignment
Channel
Top Tab

1. Select a calendar template from Genially.
2. Enter your weekly assignments, content, and announcements into the template. Use the audio feature, link to Teams assignments or links for learning, and even add hover text.

Scan this QR code to access a video on how to create calendars in Genially.

3. Add the Genially to your Team by embedding it in a Teams OneNote assignment, adding it as a Teams top tab, or posting it as an announcement or post.

Genially Play #5: Planners

Text can become overused in online instruction. Use Genially planner templates to create an eye-appealing and engaging way for students to stay on task. Create a Genially planner and embed it in your class OneNote to keep you on track, to allow for your students to plan, or to let parents know what units are being covered next.

1. Select a planner template from Genially.
2. Enter your weekly assignments, content, announcements, and important information into the template. Use the audio feature, link to Teams assignments or links for learning, and even add hover text.
3. Add the Genially to your Team by embedding it into your Teams OneNote notebook. Use it in the teacher-only section or embed it for student view in the Content Area, Collaboration Space, or in Individual Student Sections.

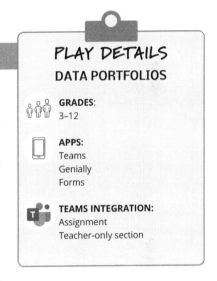

PLAY DETAILS
DATA PORTFOLIOS

GRADES:
3–12

APPS:
Teams
Genially
Forms

TEAMS INTEGRATION:
Assignment
Teacher-only section

Scan this QR code to access a video of how to make a Genially planner.

Scan this QR code to see additional Genially lessons.

Flipgrid

SCOUTING PROFILE

ACCESSIBILITY

GRADES   **PRICE**

TOP FEATURES

- Screen recording
- Whiteboard
- Flipgrid Shorts
- Text feedback
- Mic-only mode

GET CONNECTED

JENALLEE BLOG

MEC RESOURCES

Overview of Flipgrid

Flipgrid is a video platform that equips students with the ability to record video or audio responses to a topic shared by the teacher. Flipgrid camera offers students the ability to personalize videos with tools such as draw, whiteboard, emojis, frames, filters, stickers, text, etc.

When we saw Flipgrid for the first time in 2016–2017, we loved the ease, functionality, and relevance this app brought to our classrooms. Since then, Flipgrid has evolved dramatically, and what we used to call the "ultimate *selfie video* app," we now call the "ultimate *learning* app." As our friend Jornea Armant, Head of Education Innovation at Flipgrid, says, "If you can think it, you can Flipgrid it."

Using Flipgrid allows you to see and hear what your students are thinking. Students can verbally justify their thoughts, teach or reteach a concept, debate topics, pose questions, create and share video projects, and more. Flipgrid includes many learning features:

- Video (both selfie and front-facing video)
- Whiteboard
- Stickers/emojis
- Premade topics in the Discovery Library
- Videos upload
- Ability to add resources to topics
- Ability to connect with educators and classrooms around the world
- Drawing features
- Screen recording
- Editing capabilities
- Video and text feedback commenting
- Mic mode (voice-only recording)

"

"Flipgrid not only facilitates academic growth but also provides the perfect environment to nurture citizenship, both within their school community, the community they live in but most importantly global citizenship. Connecting classes through topics, pupils can share their diverse cultures, develop friendships, enjoy the things they have in common, and celebrate their differences. When we allow our pupils to make this important connection, we are providing them with an opportunity to make friends across the world and allowing them to take the first steps in being the global change makers we wish them to become."

Paul 'Lanny' Watkins (@Lanny_Watkins)

"

Flipgrid Play #1: Video Directions

Offering your students multimodal directions helps ensure all students understand the expectations for the activity. We like using Flipgrid Shorts to create short and concise directions for our students. Use the built-in screen recorder, inking, and adding images to demonstrate exactly what you want your students to accomplish. Shorts offers up to ten minutes to record stand-alone videos, and directly showing your students what to do via video is a great way to ensure they understand the activities you want them to complete.

Simply copy and paste the link of the Short to embed it and play it in the OneNote page. This is a perfect way to offer directions to students for their Teams OneNote assignments.

PLAY DETAILS

DATA PORTFOLIOS

GRADES:
K–12

APPS:
Teams
OneNote
Flipgrid

TEAMS INTEGRATION:
Assignment
OneNote Notebook
Teams Top Tab

Lesson Idea

Use Flipgrid directions as a top tab in Teams, where you can share a topic, group, or short. You can create directions for the day and post them as a top tab to help your students understand the expectations for work to be done during the day.

#Jenallee

Scan this QR code to see some of our Flipgrid Shorts direction examples.

Scan this QR code to see more from our dear friend Chris Gerrard, Digital Learning Consultant and fellow MIE Expert from Scotland.

Flipgrid Play #2: Podcast Bingo

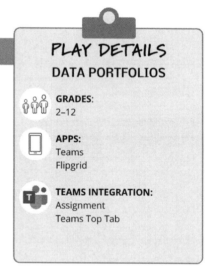

PLAY DETAILS
DATA PORTFOLIOS

GRADES:
2–12

APPS:
Teams
Flipgrid

TEAMS INTEGRATION:
Assignment
Teams Top Tab

Lesson Idea

Use Flipgrid's Mic Mode to create podcasts. Because students can record just their voices, it eliminates the fear of video recording. Students can practice authentic listening and verbally explain concepts and reflections.

Bring a little gaming into the activity by playing Podcast Bingo. Students listen to peers' podcasts, and as they hear specific aspects, they check them off on a BINGO card. They continue listening to peers' videos until someone gets a "BINGO!"

Coaches' Corner

Use Bingo for any of your Flipgrid topics. Add a few things to a BINGO card you want your students to observe, and ask them to watch their friends until they get a BINGO. This game offers students variety and is more engaging than simply watching videos or videos of their peers.

For example: If you were to use the "What's in the bag" Discovery Library topic, students can record a video sharing what is in their backpack, then use a BINGO card as they watch their peers' videos. They will continue watching videos until they are able to mark a BINGO on their card.

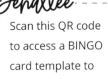

#Jenallee

Scan this QR code to access a BINGO card template to customize for your own Flipgrid Bingo.

WHAT'S INSIDE MY BAG?

Write the classmates name on an item that is in their virtual backpack. Keep watching videos until you get a Bingo! Names can only be used one time.

FREE

"Student voice is authentic and unique. When we were first introduced to Flipgrid we could immediately see this and understood how important and versatile this tool would be. When you give students the chance to speak and take ownership of their learning you will never be disappointed."

Joe & Kristin Merrill (@themerrillsedu)

Flipgrid Play #3: TikTok Videos

PLAY DETAILS

DATA PORTFOLIOS

GRADES:
3–12

APPS:
Teams
Flipgrid

TEAMS INTEGRATION:
Assignment
Channel
Top Tab

Playing popular TikTok games on Flipgrid is fun and a good way to introduce concepts, review concepts, or connect with your students. Teachers can easily incorporate this into Teams by adding the topic as a top tab or sharing the topic to Teams as an assignment or post. Below are a few game ideas you can try with your students.

"Put Down a Finger If" Tik Tok Game

Five "if" statements are asked in a video. Students record their response to the questions. They hold up five fingers and then drop a finger for each statement that pertains to them.

Teachers create a video example of "Put a Finger Down If . . ." and add it as the media for your topic. You can record it as you are creating the topic or pre-record and add the video as the media.

Students use the Flipgrid camera **record screen** feature. Students will open the TikTok example topic provided by the teacher. They will record their screen as the game plays. The student will appear in the bottom corner as they respond to each statement. Students place one finger down for each correct statement in the video. Students view each other's videos to learn about each other, connect, and have fun!

Create a Flipgrid mixtape, a collection of videos containing groups of students with the same number of lowered fingers at the end of their individual videos. For example, create a mixtape of videos in which students have only one finger remaining, one of videos with students who have two fingers remaining, etc. Students with the same number of lowered fingers can view each other's videos and comment using text or video. This is a great way for students to identify commonalities amongst their peers. You could also use this as a fun way to create groups within your classroom for activities.

"Tell Me You're a _____ Without Telling Me You're a _____."

Play this game to help students learn vocabulary words. The goal is for students to video themselves as they describe the word without using the word. If the statement was "Tell me you're a mammal without telling me you're a mammal," for example, students might say, "I am a bear, and I have fur that keeps me warm in the winter. I also have cubs that drink milk."

Students can show items, explain the word differently, or associate the word with something else.

TikTok MythBusters

Students get to debunk the myths they see in class, on TV, or on TikTok. They have one minute to explain or show a science experiment to debunk the fake news or myths they see around them.

Scan this QR code to receive a TikTok game to use with your students on Flipgrid.

Flipgrid Play #4: Classroom Culture and Relationships

Creating a classroom culture where all students are valued, loved, and understood is essential to learning. Students can't learn if they don't feel their voice is heard. Use Flipgrid to create a space to give your students a voice and a venue for their passion, and to teach them how to communicate, share, and connect with each other. Use this platform to bring awareness, understanding, empathy, and connection between students.

PLAY DETAILS
DATA PORTFOLIOS

GRADES:
2–12

APPS:
Teams
Flipgrid

TEAMS INTEGRATION:
Assignment
Channel
Top Tab

Consider including some of these topics:

- Five interesting things about me are…
- One talent I have is…
- The talent I wish I had is…
- My favorite _____ is…
- I will change the world by…
- A family tradition that is important to me is…

Scan this QR code to see additional Flipgrid lessons.

Be sure to search the Flipgrid Discovery Library for community building topics.

—— 66 ——

"The most important aspect of student engagement is having the ability to tailor specific aspects of your lesson plan or object to the individual students in your classroom. I use Flipgrid because it allows us to engage with students and families on a personal level. Culturally Responsive Pedagogy asks that we consider our students' interests, their cultural references, and their personal experiences in our daily teaching practices. Flipgrid allows for all of this. You are encouraging students to integrate the use of the camera features to create powerful products for tasks I would have assigned as essays for the course."

Yaritza Villalba (@inc_yv)

—— 99 —

Buncee

SCOUTING PROFILE

ACCESSIBILITY

GRADES   **PRICE**

TOP FEATURES

- Ease of use
- Integrated images and .gifs
- Embedded content
- Templates
- Ideas Lab
- Accessibility tools

GET CONNECTED

JENALLEE BLOG

MEC RESOURCES

Overview of Buncee

When we are asked for a creative, easy, and fun tool for students to use, Buncee is one of the first tools we suggest. Buncee is kid-friendly and great for projects, justifying thinking, practicing concepts, and more. It also includes a lot of templates created by teachers for teachers! One of the most impressive features of Buncee is its community of educators using the platform to cultivate empathy and change within their communities. Educators around the world are looking for ways to connect and work toward common goals together with their students, and Buncee is the perfect platform for this emphasis in the classroom.

"When I think of engagement, I believe that allowing students to see their thinking become a reality is the foundation of active learning. Buncee is a fantastic tool that matches student creativity with usable tools. Add a collaborative platform like Microsoft Teams, and learning efficiency goes through the roof. I have seen educators incorporate Buncee with learning opportunities like choice boards, public service announcements projects, research projects, writing brainstorming, and video playlists for remote learning practice."

Dr. Matthew X Joseph (@MatthewXJoseph)

Buncee Play #1:
Buncee + Teams Integrated Features

PLAY DETAILS
DATA PORTFOLIOS

GRADES:
3–12

APPS:
Teams
Teams Buncee App

Teams Integration:
Teams Posts
Teams Chat
Teams Assignments
Teams Meetings

Lesson Idea

Below are three different lesson ideas for using Buncee and Teams together.

Buncee Messages/Cards. Use Buncee Messages to encourage and praise students—a great way to stay connected and give feedback. Allow students to send encouraging messages to each other to foster an environment of positivity and support.

To send a Buncee message/card:

1. Click on *Posts* in the channel or the chat you want to send the message in.
2. Click on the Buncee icon under the text bar.
3. Search and select the image you would like to send.

Buncee Questioning. Add your Buncee presentation to any Teams call and ask your students questions throughout the lesson with each slide. You can use this feature for formative assessments and to check for understanding. Use this feature throughout the lesson to help drive the conversation and direct teaching content. All responses are saved in the Teams Meeting chat group and in the comments of your Buncee.

Buncee Board Top Tab. Add a Buncee Board as a top tab to see students' work when it is submitted. Buncee Boards are like digital bulletin boards. Students can post their Buncee on the board for their classmates to review and see their classmates' work on the Buncee Board in Teams.

Coaches' Corner

Activate the Buncee app by selecting Apps in the Teams me space and click **Activate.** The Buncee icon will appear under the text bar in posts and chat.

#*Jenallee*

Scan this QR code to see videos and resources about how to use Buncee messages, poll students with your Buncee presentation in a Teams Meeting, and add Buncee Boards as a top tab.

Time Out

Did you know Immersive Reader is available in Buncee? Scan this QR code to see a video explaining more.

Buncee Play #2: Collaborative Buncees

PLAY DETAILS
DATA PORTFOLIOS

GRADES:
K–12

APPS:
Teams
Buncee

TEAMS INTEGRATION:
Teams Meetings

Lesson Idea

Buncee adds fun to group work and projects. Check out this Teams and Buncee hack to promote this collaboration.

Currently, Buncee only allows one person to work actively on a shared project. Teams Meetings allow students to work collaboratively on Buncees in real time. Simply enter a meeting together, share your screen, and allow your group members the ability to control the shared screen. This allows two people to work on one person's Buncee at the same time!

#Jenallee

See how to work collaboratively on Buncees in this High Five video.

Coaches' Corner

Check out the clip and stitch feature for combining Buncees.

Buncee Play #3: Class Meeting Slides

PLAY DETAILS
DATA PORTFOLIOS

GRADES:
K–12

APPS:
Teams
Buncee

TEAMS INTEGRATION:
Teams Meetings

Lesson Idea

Use Buncee to create class meeting slides for your Teams Meetings. Include important information such as a countdown timer, bell work, etiquette, needed supplies, and more!

Buncees are graphically appealing and interactive. They allow the teacher to embed different types of content and easily share it with students for independent practice. During a Teams Meeting, students can see the content, participate in polls, and individually practice the concepts being taught.

Buncee can be used for the following tasks:

- Class agendas
- Greeting slides with directions, welcome activities, or a countdown timer
- Bell work
- Work for each subject with links to videos, creation tools, etc.
- Your teaching corner
- Recorded directions (using Buncee video or audio)

#Jenallee

Scan this QR code for access to editable templates for Buncee Meeting Slides. Sign in to Buncee and click **copy**.

Buncee Play #4: Buncee and Teams Meetings

Lesson Idea

If you are not using Teams as your LMS, or are using only Teams Meetings with your students, Buncee makes it easy to create and connect with them through Teams. You can schedule a Teams Meeting from the Buncee dashboard and easily share it.

Follow these steps to get started:

1. Log in to your Buncee account
2. Click on the Teams icon at the top of your Buncee dashboard
3. Create and share with your students
4. Teams chat is saved in the Buncee as comments

Buncee and Teams together gives you the power to:

- Share your Buncee through the Teams Meeting
- Question students on Buncee slides in the meetings (Teams chat is saved in the Buncee as comments)
- Create Buncee task cards for Teams break-out rooms
- Engage students in collaborative work on Buncee projects while connected on Teams

PLAY DETAILS
DATA PORTFOLIOS

GRADES:
3–12

APPS:
Teams
Buncee

TEAMS INTEGRATION:
Teams Meetings

#Jenallee

Scan this QR code to view a quick how-to video for setting up your Teams Meeting in Buncee.

Buncee Play #5: Buncee Embeddable Designs

Lesson Idea

Use Buncee in your Teams OneNote Class Notebook. You can create:

- Headers for each section
- Calendars
- PDF worksheets
- Announcements
- Lesson plans
- A computer desktop
- Buncee choice boards

You can easily share this content with your students as a OneNote Class Notebook assignment. Copy and paste your Buncee share link into the OneNote page you would like to assign, and the Buncee will embed. Assign this page through your Teams Assignment.

PLAY DETAILS
DATA PORTFOLIOS

GRADES:
3–12

APPS:
Teams
Buncee
OneNote

TEAMS INTEGRATION:
Teams OneNote
Notebooks
Teams Top Tab
Teams Meetings

Scan this QR code to learn how to embed a Buncee into OneNote.

"Buncee truly makes me to feel like my most creative self. As an instructional coach and technology integration mentor, I love to use it for creating district and campus signage, graphics for presentations and announcements, and just recently I used it to create my very own computer desktop background. The possibilities are endless!"

Amy Storer (@techamys)

Buncee Play #6: Buncee Teams Breakout Cards

PLAY DETAILS
DATA PORTFOLIOS

GRADES:
K–12

APPS:
Teams
OneNote
Buncee

TEAMS INTEGRATION:
Teams OneNote Notebooks
Teams Top Tab
Teams Meetings

Lesson Idea

Create Breakout cards to help your students learn, work together, and be productive. To make them, simply

1. Create task cards for your Teams breakout groups.
2. Share the Buncee Breakout Cards with each Teams breakout group.
3. Students work together to complete the tasks.
4. Post a Buncee Board to a Teams top tab to see student work.
5. Teachers can jump from breakout group to breakout group to guide students in their work.

Consider including the following items on your Buncee Breakout Cards:

- Student jobs/roles (recorder, reporter, timekeeper, researcher, special effects director, director, etc.)
- Objective (Use audio recording or video recording built into Buncee to record their task.)
- Links to work within the Buncee

You can embed the cards in the OneNote Class Notebook for students to easily locate as a Teams assignment. You can also add the Buncee as a Teams top tab in the group channel for one student to work on.

#Jenallee

Scan this QR code to receive editable Buncee Breakout card templates.

Buncee Play #7: Buncee Choice Boards

Lesson Idea

Choice boards fit perfectly into the Explore section of the HyperDoc lesson cycle. Use Buncee to design choice boards for students to choose among videos, articles, interactive tutorials, virtual field trips, or any other number of resources at their fingertips. They are interactive, engaging, and easy to share, and they allow students to explore content in a way that best fits their learning needs.

Follow these steps to create choice boards in Buncee quickly:

1. Create new Buncee.
2. Select a background. You can search for something to match the theme of your unit, bulletin boards, classrooms, etc. Select a background that allows you to customize a page that is easy to explore and to locate information.
3. Link and embed your learning content.
4. Share the content:

    a. Send to Teams from the social button.
    b. Copy the link and share as a top tab in Teams.
    c. Copy and paste the link into a Teams OneNote Class Notebook page.

PLAY DETAILS

DATA PORTFOLIOS

 GRADES:
2–12

 APPS:
Teams
OneNote
Buncee

 Teams Integration:
Teams OneNote Notebooks
Teams Top Tab
Teams Assignment

 Coaches' Corner

Bring some fun to your class by uploading your Bitmojis (customizable cartoon avatars) into Buncee. If you add the Bitmoji extension, you can copy the image URL of your chosen Bitmoji and paste it into the Import URL option on the Buncee creation canvas. Scan this QR code to view a quick tutorial video.

 #*Jenallee*

 Scan this QR code to access Buncee choice board templates.

 Scan this QR code to see additional Buncee lessons.

"Buncee has been a game changer for libraries. In addition to creating new signage, I use Buncee to create printable bookmarks to share with students. I also use it for my virtual library, showcasing books I have read with links to book trailers and author interviews. Being able to create a classroom and have students create unlimited Buncees has been great. I also created Podcast Choice boards and college research projects. One of my former students has even written a blog for Buncee."

Deb Zeman (@DebZemanLMS)

Adobe Spark

SCOUTING PROFILE

ACCESSIBILITY

GRADES   **PRICE**

TOP FEATURES

- Creates polished content
- Easy to create videos, webpages, and graphics
- Templates
- Remix
- Send to Teams

GET CONNECTED

JENALLEE BLOG

MEC RESOURCES

Overview of Adobe Spark

Add a little "spark" to your lessons! Easily create graphics, videos, and websites with Adobe Spark, where beautiful images, graphics, and powerful tools are built in. Adobe's reputation as a powerhouse of creation does not disappoint. Wonderful images, eye-appealing templates, and ease of use are all encompassed within this creation suite. Take it a step further and speak with your technology department about integrating Adobe Spark into your school's Single Sign On (SSO) for restriction-free access.

"Adobe Spark gives learners advanced digital tools to create professional looking videos, portfolios, journals, and graphics to tell their stories. It allows them to focus on the content and not worry about the technical aspects of the tools."

Claudio Zavala (@ClaudioZavalaJr)

Adobe Spark Play #1: SMART Goals

PLAY DETAILS
DATA PORTFOLIOS

GRADES:
1–12

APPS:
Teams
Adobe Spark
OneNote

TEAMS INTEGRATION:
Assignment

Lesson Idea

Adobe Spark has pre-created templates and worksheets, and one of our favorites is SMART (specific, measurable, attainable, relevant, and time-based) goals! We highly recommend setting SMART goals with your students and exploring their needs and obstacles.

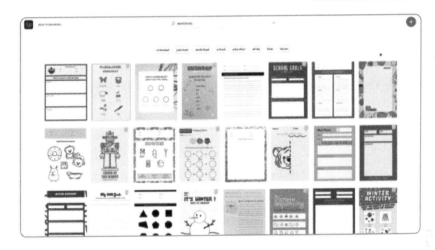

The following is a breakdown of how to create the SMART goals:

1. Log in to Adobe Spark. Use the search bar at the top of the screen to search for SMART Goals.

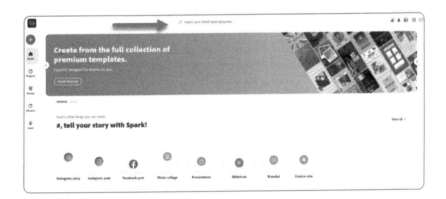

2. Peruse the collection of SMART Goals Worksheets and select the one you want to use. You can also edit the template to make it specific for your students. Download the design as a PDF.

3. Upload the worksheet to your OneNote Class Notebook. Click **Insert** and then **Insert Printout**. (We like to create in the "Teacher Only" section and then distribute or assign work from this location.)

4. Right click on the PDF image and set PDF as a background.

5. Go to Teams Assignments and assign this page from your OneNote Class Notebook for your students to complete.

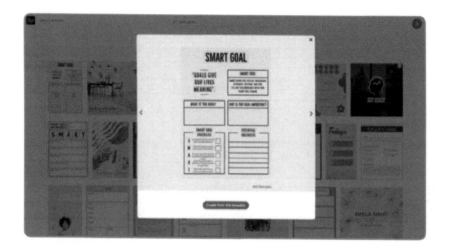

We also use Spark to create digital data binders through our Teams OneNote Class Notebooks. Using premade templates from Adobe makes these binders engaging, easy to complete, and effective in measuring goals and data. Using Adobe Spark Templates and Teams OneNote Class Notebooks, students can type, draw, dictate, or leave audio messages summarizing their thoughts on the Adobe Spark Post embedded in OneNote.

#Jenallee

Scan this QR code to remix our favorite premade Adobe Spark SMART Goals template.

Coaches' Corner

Delete the inserted PDF icon from the OneNote so students type directly in the OneNote and not in the PDF.

Adobe Spark Play #2: Semester Exam Portfolios

PLAY DETAILS
DATA PORTFOLIOS

GRADES:
3–12

APPS:
Teams
Adobe Spark

TEAMS INTEGRATION:
Teams Assignment

Lesson Idea

We are excited to share this idea from Trevor MacKenzie! Check out his Tweet, and follow him on Twitter: @Trev_mackenzie.

Trevor MacKenzie
@trev_mackenzie

This week I wrote my report cards with my students.

Our final exam was a reflection conversation about their learning & their growth.

We discussed challenges they faced, strategies they utilized, highlights of their learning & competency development.

Time well spent ✦

11:08 PM · Nov 13, 2020 · Twitter for iPhone

44 Retweets   **17** Quote Tweets   **388** Likes

To expand on this idea, encourage students to evaluate their SMART goals and use Adobe Spark Pages to create a student portfolio showcasing their best work and summarizing their growth. They can bring the portfolio to their final exam conference. To complete the portfolio, students create a website with Adobe Spark, where they can add images, videos, and text to highlight their work.

Here's how students create an Adobe Spark Page:

1. Log in to Adobe Spark and click on the plus button and select **Web Page**.
2. Use the plus button to insert SMART goals and share reflections on challenges faced, strategies used, and updated goals for the next six weeks.
3. Copy published link and submit link to Teams Assignment.

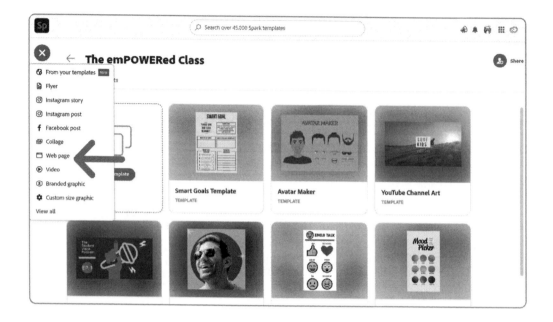

Adobe Spark Play #3: Create Custom Teams Announcement Headers

Lesson Idea

Create your own custom Teams Announcement Headers with Adobe Spark! Announcements bring attention to your Teams Posts, and Teams has many premade graphics for you to choose from. If you prefer to customize your content, you can create your own with Adobe.

Here are a few theme ideas:

- Bitmoji headers
- Subject area
- Announcements
- Units of study
- Daily learning schedules

PLAY DETAILS

DATA PORTFOLIOS

GRADES:
K–12

APPS:
Teams
Adobe Spark

TEAMS INTEGRATION:
Teams Announcement Post

Here's how to create a custom header:

1. Go to Adobe Spark and create a Spark Post.
2. Use the custom dimensions 918 × 120 px.
3. Download your creation.
4. Go to your Team and Start a New Conversation.
5. Click on the format icon and select **Announcement**.
6. Select the image icon on the far right: on the Teams header, select **custom**.
7. Upload your Adobe Spark creation as your new Teams header.

Scan this QR code to see a video on how to create a custom Teams Announcement header using Adobe Spark.

Adobe Spark Play #4: Emoji Talk

Lesson Idea

Emojis are not just fun; they catch your eye, are engaging, and help students remember information. This makes them *educational*! Below are six emoji lessons you can adapt to fit the learning unit you are working on.

Emoji Talk SEL: Help your students evaluate their social and emotional status each day. Post the Emoji Talk image as a Teams Announcement. Students can respond to the announcement with the emoji that reflects their emotions for the day. You can also add this activity as a OneNote Class Notebook Assignment.

Emoji Character Analysis: After reading a story, ask students to decide which emoji fits each character. Add a remix link to a Teams Assignment or insert the PDF in a OneNote Teams Assignment.

Emoji Formative Assessment: Use this graphic for formative assessment as students reflect on their understanding after a unit of study. Add the image or PDF to a OneNote assignment so that students can use the Draw tool to indicate their knowledge.

PLAY DETAILS
DATA PORTFOLIOS

GRADES:
3–12

APPS:
Teams
OneNote
Adobe Spark

TEAMS INTEGRATION:
Teams Assignment
Teams Announcement
Teams Top Tab
OneNote Assignment

Emoji Response Rubric for Teams Meeting: Use this Adobe creation as a rubric for student responses during direct teaching in a Teams Meeting. Share the image in the meeting chat so that students can be reminded of the meaning of emojis for responding in a Teams Meeting.

Emoji Talk in Teams Posts: Provide a rubric for emoji responses in Teams Posts. Students can reply to Teams Posts and announcements with emojis indicating a specific meaning according to the provided rubric.

All About Me Emoji Challenge: Use this Adobe template to build classroom culture and get to know your students. Challenge students to describe themselves with emojis only! Ask students to record a video on Adobe Spark explaining their emoji selections.

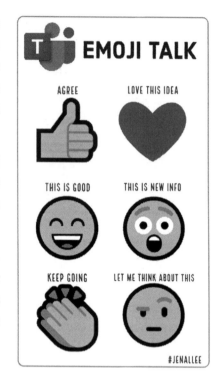

 **Coaches' Corner**

Here are tips for adding Adobe Spark creations to your OneNote Class Notebooks and Teams Assignments:

* Insert the PDF in the Teams OneNote Class Notebook. Right click and set it as a background so that students can use the draw tool. Assign this page as a Teams Assignment.

* Add the Adobe Spark Remix link to an Assignment, and students can remix the creation to show how they feel.

#Jenallee

Scan this QR code to gain access to the Emoji talk template for these lesson ideas. Remix this template to fit your lesson and activities.

Adobe Spark Play #5: Social Media Posts

PLAY DETAILS
DATA PORTFOLIOS

GRADES:
3–12

APPS:
Teams
Adobe Spark

TEAMS INTEGRATION:
Assignment

Lesson Idea

Social media posts are a great way to connect to a relevant application of knowledge. Students can demonstrate their knowledge of content in a way relevant to their everyday lives.

The following are a few examples of social media post ideas using premade templates available in Adobe Spark.

- My Top 10
- Never Have I Ever
- This or That
- 5 Things I Always Say
- All About Me
- Mood Picker
- Mood Board
- My FAVS in Gifs
- 2 Truths and a Lie

You can use any of these templates to build community in your classroom, reflect on a unit being taught, and relate to a character in a story or a historical figure, and so forth. Offer your students the ability to use their creativity to demonstrate their knowledge.

#Jenallee

Scan this QR code to gain access to a variety of remix social media templates.

Scan this QR code to see additional Adobe Spark lessons.

Wakelet

SCOUTING PROFILE

ACCESSIBILITY

GRADES

Student Creation: 13+
Teacher Use: K–12

PRICE

TOP FEATURES

- Organize content easily
- Visually appealing
- Collaborative
- Easily shared
- Multimedia integrations
- Spaces
- Immersive Reader

GET CONNECTED

JENALLEE BLOG

MEC RESOURCES

Overview of Wakelet

Wakelet is a content creation platform, immersing students in various learning opportunities. They can collaborate, curate, create, communicate, and so much more, all from within this one platform. Whether they create websites, answer formative assessment questions, engage in discussions, create blog posts, or curate research content, students and educators can easily share their creations with the world.

 Coaches' Corner

Scan this QR code to read a blog post by Holly Clark, as she shares a variety of ways to use Wakelet in the classroom.

"Wakelet is a power tool for educators and students alike! There are an infinity of ways to use it in the classroom: student or teacher portfolios to showcase progress and creativity, self-paced lessons to encourage learner autonomy, back channels for communication, research curation for critical thinking and so much more! You'll never regret learning and utilizing Wakelet!"

Tisha Poncio (@TxTechChick)

Wakelet Play #1: Wakelet Tutorials

Lesson Idea

Provide examples, directions and tutorials for your students to access anytime while learning. Use Wakelet to create tutorials to clarify concepts taught, expectations, directions for completing tasks, etc. This information can be used by students and parents for a more enriching learning experience.

PLAY DETAILS
DATA PORTFOLIOS

GRADES:
K–12

APPS:
Teams
Wakelet

TEAMS INTEGRATION:
Teams Top Tab
Teams Assignments
Teams Post

- Provide step-by-step typed instructions or include video directions for students about how to operate technology, complete a math problem, or even how to successfully turn in work. You also can create instructions for parents about activities you are doing in class that they can do at home with their child to better create that home–school connection.

- Add tutorials to a Wakelet Space or Collection and curate tutorials for students and parents.

- Create a channel for tutorials in Teams. Add a top tab with the Wakelet Collection or Space link for students to easily reference.

This gives you the ability to build your own tutorial library for your students and parents to access at any time from a computer, tablet, or mobile device.

Scan this QR code to see tips and tricks for how to create tutorials in Wakelet.

Scan this QR code to see how our friend Chris Gerrard, Digital Learning Consultant and fellow MIE Expert from Scotland, uses Wakelet.

Wakelet Play #2: Wakelet Assessments

PLAY DETAILS

DATA PORTFOLIOS

GRADES:
4–12

APPS:
Teams
Wakelet

TEAMS INTEGRATION:
Teams Top Tab
Teams Assignment
Teams Post
Teams Class
OneNote Notebook

Lesson Idea

Assess your students' knowledge of content by using Wakelet collaborations in an Exit Ticket situation. Invite your students, through a contributor link, to add text, video, links, and more to your Wakelet. This quick assessment of student knowledge can direct you as you facilitate further explanation and quality discussions, and it will provide guidance for future lessons. To use this idea, simply

1. Copy the contributor link and add it as a Teams top tab, Teams post, or Teams assignment to allow students to contribute to the Wakelet.

2. Ask your students to answer the questions in the Wakelet as they exit class. This provides a quick assessment of their knowledge of the concepts being taught.

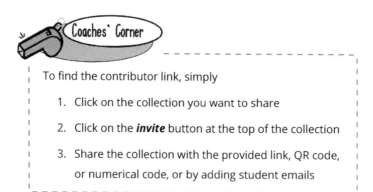

Coaches' Corner

To find the contributor link, simply

1. Click on the collection you want to share

2. Click on the **invite** button at the top of the collection

3. Share the collection with the provided link, QR code, or numerical code, or by adding student emails

The same idea can be applied to summative portfolios in which students curate their best work in a Wakelet for a summative assessment. They can explain concepts learned, share their quality pieces of work, reflect on their work, and share their goals for learning. Through a collaborator link, you can leave feedback and praise throughout the portfolio.

"

"The society has shifted from a lack of access to information forty years ago, to having access to too much information. Curating the information we find online is one of the biggest challenges we face nowadays as a society. These skills need to be taught in the classroom for students to be successful in their future. Wakelet is the perfect tool for this purpose. Students and teachers can curate and organize their content in different collections."

eTwinz (Mario & AlbertoHerraez @eTwinzEDU)

"

Wakelet Play #3: Wakelet Classroom Space

Lesson Idea

Seamlessly curate and build content for your students, and organize content, resources, and units of study within Wakelet. Partnered with Teams, your classroom is an organizational masterpiece. Students can easily access the content within their Team that you have organized or that has been crowdsourced by students. Wakelet allows the teacher to scaffold content or encourage collaboration and shared resources to drive student learning.

Implement this idea with three easy steps:

1. Create a Wakelet Space with collection of content that you want your students to access.

2. Add the collections with your desired input, either teacher-curated or student-sourced. Within Spaces, you can add Wakelet Collections. If you want to be the only contributor to the Wakelet collection, copy and paste the view link for that collection into the Wakelet Space. For student-driven collections, copy and paste the contributor link for that collection into the Wakelet Space.

3. Add the Wakelet Space link as a top tab within the Teams channel of your choice.

PLAY DETAILS
DATA PORTFOLIOS

GRADES:
3–12

APPS:
Teams
Wakelet

TEAMS INTEGRATION:
Teams Private Channel
OneNote Class Notebook
Student Section
Teams Assignment

 Coaches' Corner

When adding a Wakelet collection as a Teams top tab, we suggest you add it with the Wakelet App integration. If you add it as a Wakelet Space to your Teams top tab, we suggest adding it as a website.

#Jenallee

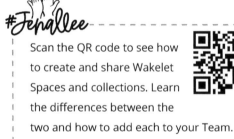

Scan the QR code to see how to create and share Wakelet Spaces and collections. Learn the differences between the two and how to add each to your Team.

Wakelet Play #4: Wakelet Portfolios

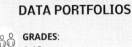

PLAY DETAILS
DATA PORTFOLIOS

 GRADES:
4–12

 APPS:
Teams
Wakelet
OneNote

 TEAMS INTEGRATION:
OneNote Class Notebook
Student Section
Teams Assignment

Lesson Idea

Create Wakelet student portfolios to showcase student work, goals set and reached, and student reflections. Encourage students to save their work in one place so it can be shared easily with anyone they choose. Students can include text, published articles, produced videos, resumes, personal information, and more. Wakelet makes it easy to share the content with anyone through an email, link, or even a QR code.

Provide your students with a template so they know exactly what is required. The template allows them to simply fill in the necessary parts of the portfolio.

Scan this QR code to see examples of Wakelet portfolio templates you can use with your students.

"As a teacher with dyslexia myself, I see the need for having these tools available for my students. Wakelet is an amazing tool that allows students to actually see their growth and effort. I use it in my art classes with photography and themes. Allowing written reflection with images helps the teacher to see what the students are trying to do even if they are not successful. Accessibility is built into Wakelet with Immersive Reader. When students use the Edge browser, it helps them to better understand what is being asked by having it read aloud."

Pamela Spangler (@ArtySpangles)

Wakelet Play #5: Wakelet Collections in Posts

PLAY DETAILS

DATA PORTFOLIOS

GRADES:
4–12

APPS:
Teams
Wakelet

TEAMS INTEGRATION:
Teams Channel Posts

Lesson Idea

We love being able to save links from a Teams post conversation directly to a Wakelet. The links can connect to assignments, articles, forms, videos, etc. Not only can you save content from a conversation to a Wakelet, but you can also share Wakelets you own to a conversation post within Wakelet.

Here are the steps to enable Wakelet:

1. Click on *Apps* in the bottom left corner in the me space of Teams.
2. Search for Wakelet.
3. Click *Add*.
4. You will now see the Wakelet icon in your Teams post conversation window.

Here's how to save links to Wakelet:

1. Click the three dots in top right corner of the post you want to save to Wakelet.
2. Click on *More Actions*.
3. Click on *Save to Wakelet*.
4. Log in to your account and select the Wakelet you want to save the post to.

To share to Wakelet, simply follow these steps:

1. Click on *New Conversation*.
2. Click on the Wakelet icon in the Teams post conversation window.
3. Search your Wakelet collections for the collection you wish to share.
4. Click the airplane ("send") icon to share with your class.

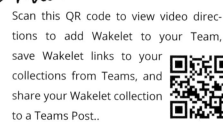

#*Jenallee*

Scan this QR code to view video directions to add Wakelet to your Team, save Wakelet links to your collections from Teams, and share your Wakelet collection to a Teams Post..

Time Out

Scan this QR code to view the Jenallee webinar "Wakelet & Microsoft Teams: Double Impact!"

Scan this QR code to see additional Wakelet lessons.

PowerPoint

Overview of PowerPoint

Some people may think PowerPoint is flat, dead, or outdated, but we are here to tell you it is very much alive and better than ever! PowerPoint offers you the ability to create stunning presentations. It also gives you the ability to practice the presentations and interact with your students in real time as you present content to your class.

Don't go any further without watching this video about PowerPoint Live Presentations! Scan this QR code to see what this *new* feature can do for you and your students.

66

"The great thing about the newest versions of PowerPoint is that your slideshows don't have to look like typical PowerPoint! With the new morph transition, support for 3D objects, zoom slides, and design ideas, users can easily make PowerPoint presentations that look like no one else's. After a close look at these new features, people say, "I didn't know you could do that in PowerPoint!"

Craig McBain (@CraigMcBain)

PowerPoint Play #1: Learning Schedule

PLAY DETAILS
DATA PORTFOLIOS

GRADES:
3–12

APPS:
Teams
PowerPoint

TEAMS INTEGRATION:
Teams Top Tab

Lesson Idea

Students can use PowerPoint to follow the daily learning schedule and locate current activities. Students use the embedded PowerPoint slides to navigate easily to their work at the assigned time.

The directions for this are simple:

1. Teacher adds an interlinked PowerPoint to a Teams Channel top tab. Click the plus button at the top of Teams, click **PowerPoint**, and select the PowerPoint of choice.

2. Students use the PowerPoint to navigate to the lesson. Click the image and advance in the PowerPoint to the slide where their activity is located.

Coaches' Corner

To interlink a PowerPoint, you will highlight the words or image you want linked, select **Ctrl+K** on your keyboard, then click on the slide in the document that you want to link to the highlighted content. Scan this QR code to see a tutorial video on how to interlink slides.

If you want your PowerPoint to play automatically when it appears in Teams, this QR code also offers a Jenallee video with directions on how to add a link extension to ensure the PowerPoint is in auto play mode in the Teams top tab.

#Jenallee

Scan this QR code for an editable PowerPoint schedule template.

PowerPoint Play #2: Bitmoji Classroom

PLAY DETAILS

DATA PORTFOLIOS

GRADES:
K–12

APPS:
Teams
PowerPoint

TEAMS INTEGRATION:
Teams Top Tab

Lesson Idea

Students can use a PowerPoint Bitmoji digital classroom to complete activities in Teams. They use PowerPoint as a top tab in Teams to navigate easily to the needed content within their digital classroom.

Teacher adds an interlinked PowerPoint to a Teams Channel top tab. Students use the PowerPoint to navigate to the lesson, books, learning activities, etc. Simply link each image to content on pages within the PowerPoint. When students click the image, the PowerPoint will advance to the slide where their activity is located.

#Jenallee

Scan the QR code to see an editable template that includes a prebuilt classroom for you to use. Simply insert your Bitmoji.

PowerPoint Play #3: Collaborative PowerPoint

PLAY DETAILS

DATA PORTFOLIOS

GRADES:
4–12

APPS:
Teams
PowerPoint

TEAMS INTEGRATION:
Teams Top Tab in private or standard channels

Lesson Idea

Use PowerPoint to create collaborative creations such as poems and stories, or to justify concepts. Students collaborate to create a project together by using PowerPoint inside their Teams channels. To implement this idea:

1. Teacher creates Teams private or standard channels for student groups.
2. Teacher will add a PowerPoint or PowerPoint template to each channel.
3. Each student group works together to create a PowerPoint project with the provided template in Teams.

Our coworker and friend Bob Eikenberry facilitated a PowerPoint project in Teams with some of our teachers to bring two classrooms from two different schools together to create a story within PowerPoint. While using Teams Meetings and Chat, students collaborated to create a PowerPoint about a water droplet's journey through the water cycle.

Bob explained the students benefited because each student group was able to explain and teach the concepts, while justifying their thoughts about the order of their water cycle story. In turn, each group also heard the concepts explained in different ways and could compare those ideas with their own to determine why the story needed to be written in a certain order.

The teachers also benefited because they were able to jump into each channel to hear and see what the students were teaching and thinking, and to explain concepts in different ways. They also could guide student thinking with questions designed to steer them to correct conclusions.

For more ideas from Bob Eikenberry, follow him on Twitter: @BobEikenberry

PowerPoint Play #4: Choice Boards

Lesson Idea

Easily create choice boards with PowerPoint. Link icons and online images to teaching websites and apps such as Flipgrid, Wakelet, Gale, Pebble Go, YouTube Videos, Quizlet flashcards, online articles, PDFs, and more. Make your choice boards come to life by including these features:

PLAY DETAILS

DATA PORTFOLIOS

GRADES:
K –12

APPS:
Teams
PowerPoint

TEAMS INTEGRATION:
Teams Top Tab
Teams Assignments
OneNote Assignments

- **PowerPoint Screen Recorder.** Use PowerPoint screen recording to record directions for your students.
- **Designer.** Use the Designer to choose from designed slides with your content.
- **Interlink Your Slides.** If you don't want your students to leave PowerPoint, add content to each slide and link them back to the choice board item on the main slide.

Students can use your Choice Board PowerPoint to explore content in an attempt to answer the driving question for the lesson. Offer students the opportunity to reflect on their learning after they explore by giving them a link to Flipgrid or Wakelet, or by asking them to type their thoughts into the final slide of the PowerPoint. You can then share the choice board with your students as a top tab in a Teams channel, Teams assignment, or as a Teams post.

#Jenallee

Scan this QR code to access a Wakelet collection that includes our editable templates that contain PowerPoint pages with premade choice board layouts. Simply add your links to create appealing learning content for your students.

PowerPoint Play #5: Direct Teach with Replay

Replay is an application that will replay all of your inking in a PowerPoint. To use this function, follow these steps:

1. Click the **Draw** menu.
2. Select a pen and ink in the PowerPoint.
3. Click the **View** menu.
4. Select the lasso tool and lasso the content you want replayed.
5. Click on **Replay**.

Replay will play the content you selected exactly as you inked it on the page.

PLAY DETAILS

DATA PORTFOLIOS

GRADES:
4–12

APPS:
Teams
PowerPoint

TEAMS INTEGRATION:
Teams Top Tab
Teams Post

Lesson Idea

During class, directly teach concepts from PowerPoint. You can fully illustrate the content by inking on the slides so students can better understand it. For example, while teaching long division, you can ink a problem within PowerPoint while explaining how to complete the problem. During independent work time, students can use the Replay feature to see the problem reworked, stroke by stroke, on the page.

Add this PowerPoint as a top tab in Teams or in a OneNote Class Notebook for students to access easily and view the class notes.

#Jenallee

Scan this QR code to see videos of Replay in action in PowerPoint and OneNote.

Scan this QR code to see additional PowerPoint lessons.

Canva

SCOUTING PROFILE

ACCESSIBILITY

GRADES   **PRICE**

TOP FEATURES

- Visually appealing graphics, presentations, and videos
- Collaborative documents
- Templates
- Virtual Classroom Kits
- App integration
- Get Connected

GET CONNECTED

JENALLEE BLOG

MEC RESOURCES

Overview of Canva

Yes, you *can* create with *Canva*! Bringing an amazing "wow" factor to each creation, this online tool offers educators and students a world of creative options! With templates for Instagram, TikTok, virtual classrooms, worksheets, and more, you may find yourself obsessed with this new tool! Creators who like using templates and those who like to create from scratch will all love Canva. Students' demonstration of learning comes to life with advanced creation tools such as background removal, video recording, animation, filters, and more. Students *and* teachers can create, edit a shared template, and collaborate with this app. Sharing creation templates makes team planning a breeze. Send your lessons to other teachers to use and stay organized by filing your creations in folders. There are free personal accounts, pro accounts, and free educator accounts.

> **"**
>
> "Using Canva in the classroom has really allowed students to get excited about what is being shared during lessons. Students are readily awaiting to find out what new fancy graphic, activity, or effects have been added to the presentation for the day, even the learning targets! Canva has helped change the boring dull slideshows into something fun and engaging for the kids."
>
> Amanda Pair (EMS ISD elem teacher)
>
> **"**

Coaches' Corner

Canva for Education is *free* for educators! Check out this Microsoft Educator Center Course titled Create and Collaborate with Canva for Education and Microsoft EDU. See an overview of the different tools, templates, and classroom features that Canva offers. You will learn how to sign up for your *free* education account, how to create classes, how to share assignments to Teams, and so much more.

Canva Play #1: SEL Check

Lesson Idea

Learning is directly linked to students' social, emotional, and physical well-being. Students need each aspect to be understood and addressed throughout the school day, so they are as healthy as possible. For this lesson idea, we created a Canva poster with social and emotional activities. Students can use the linked poster to access activities such as yoga and meditation.

This template was already created in Canva; we simply rearranged a few of the emoticons and pictures and added our own flair. Throughout each day, students can look at this poster and take a moment to reflect on their emotions. But we want to also give them tools to improve their mood and lift their spirits, so we added links to the emoticons, including links to Headspace meditations, yoga activities, and fun dance games.

You can add a linked Canva SEL activity to Teams in three easy steps:

PLAY DETAILS
DATA PORTFOLIOS

GRADES:
3–12

APPS:
Teams
Canva

TEAMS INTEGRATION:
Teams Top Tab

Coaches' Corner

If you want to take it up a notch, add new content anytime, and the view link will automatically update! Scan the QR code below for a copy of this SEL lesson template.

1. Copy the View link from the Canva SEL creation.
2. Go to Teams and click on the channel you want to place the SEL Check in.
3. Select the plus button and add the Canva link as a website.

Students can access this content anytime they need a moment to calm down, process, or breathe throughout the day.

Canva Play #2: The New Virtual Classroom

PLAY DETAILS
DATA PORTFOLIOS

GRADES:
3–12

APPS:
Teams
Canva

TEAMS INTEGRATION:
Teams Assignment
Teams Top Tab

Say goodbye to Bitmoji classroom and hello to Canva Classroom Kits! Take your virtual classroom to the next level with Canva as you easily create virtual classrooms with links to content, text, and videos. Select your colors, decor, and theme by scrolling through Canva's pre-made templates.

You also can create a lesson plan, calendar, presentation, Teams Announcement banners, and even OneNote headers with the same theme each day, week, month, or unit—all your choice.

Still want your Bitmoji in the classroom? Just use the Bitmoji add-in in Canva! Simply click on **More** on the left toolbar and select **Bitmoji.** Sign into Snapchat and—*voila*! All of your Bitmoji images will flood in. Select the one you want to add to your classroom.

Here's how to use virtual classrooms in Teams:

Coaches' Corner

Are you worried about accessibility? Remember that Microsoft Edge will read any website to students. Make sure to label your content for the reader as you build your virtual classroom.

1. Create your Canva virtual classroom presentation.
2. Add the virtual classroom as a top tab in the channel of your choice.
    *   Click on the channel.
    *   Click on the plus button.
    *   Click **Website** and paste the view link from the Canva virtual classroom creation.

If you add all of your resources and content for your students in Teams, your top tabs and channels could become numerous. By embedding them into the stylish and engaging virtual classroom you create, you can minimize the top tabs and channels your students must navigate.

#Jenallee

Scan this QR code to access a template to help you build a virtual classroom.

Canva Play #3: Comic Strip

PLAY DETAILS

DATA PORTFOLIOS

GRADES:
3–12

APPS:
Teams
Canva

TEAMS INTEGRATION:
Teams Assignment
Teams Top Tab
Teams Post

Lesson Idea

Comic strips are a fun way to retell stories, create new endings to favorite books, show the power of onomatopoeia, and more! Canva has *many* comic strip templates pre-created with characters, backgrounds, themes, and boxes or bubbles. Students select a theme and fill in the speech bubbles.

Every template includes a character theme sheet. You can change the color scheme of the image, background, or items and add more pages.

Offer this activity as group work and let students gather in Teams Meetings breakout rooms to create collaboratively in Canva. The groups can share their work in Teams Posts, and students cheer each other on in their learning!

Coaches' Corner

Search for "Comic Strip" in the Canva top search bar to locate a variety of comic strip templates to customize.

#Jenallee

Scan this QR code to see an example of a Canva comic strip design and template.

Canva Play #4: Recorded Lesson

PLAY DETAILS

DATA PORTFOLIOS

GRADES:
K–12

APPS:
Teams

TEAMS INTEGRATION:
Teams Assignment
Teams Top Tab
Teams Post

Lesson Idea

Ensuring all students receive adequate instruction in your remote and hybrid classroom days can be difficult. Providing instruction only once and reteaching only once may not be enough for some students. You can address this challenge by creating engaging presentations in Canva and then recording your lessons for your students. This offers *all* students the ability to access content when they need it— either for instruction or for review.

Follow these steps to create recorded lessons in Canva:

1. Create a presentation in Canva, using one of its appealing templates or create a presentation from scratch.
2. Click on the three dots in the top right corner and select ***Present and Record***.

Teams App Smash

Follow these steps when sharing your screen in Teams:

1. With your Canva presentation open in Canva, Click on the three dots in the top right corner.
2. Click on Present and Record.
3. Begin teaching.
4. Students in your Teams Meeting will be able to view you in the bottom corner of your presentation.
5. Canva records your presentation as you teach. After you conclude the lesson, save the Canva recording, and share it in Teams for your asynchronous learners to view.

Coaches' Corner

The following tips come from Canva.com, and we think they are fantastic!

* Easily present multiple presentations by adding them to a Playlist. Create a folder of the presentations you want to share, then present the folder.

* When presenting, press the following shortcuts on your keyboard for magic effects:

    * **Letter C** for confetti rain

    * **Letter D** for a drumroll animation

    * **Letter O** for floating bubbles

    * **Letter Q** for quiet

    * **Letter B** to blur the current slide

    * **Any number** for a timer (1 for one minute, 2 for two minutes, etc.)

* You can also press **Shift** and **?** on your keyboard to open the magic effects menu.

* To exit presentation mode, press **ESC** on your keyboard.

Canva Play #5:
The New Teacher Go-To Creation Zone

PLAY DETAILS
DATA PORTFOLIOS

GRADES:
3–12

APPS:
Teams
OneNote
Canva

TEAMS INTEGRATION:
Teams Assignment
Teams Post
Teams Top Tab

Lesson Idea

In the past, Jeni was the more organized of us, keeping every paper in order and every form signed—and keeping our calendar always up to date. I (Salleé) was the more creative one—which meant I lost every paper I touched and had to ask Jeni which appointment was next.

But today, both of us are organized and in style with Canva and OneNote! Jeni introduced me (Salleé) to OneNote about five years ago, and my world was forever changed. I can stay organized online with OneNote, and I love it! Jeni and I have many joint OneNotes, where we can share our strengths together in one space.

I (Salleé) have always dreamed of using one of the cute planners all of the other teachers used. I would buy them and cherish them—for a day. Then I would lose it, find it a month later, and then lose it again. But now I use these beautiful Canva designs and embed them in my OneNote, and I don't lose them!

#Jenallee

Scan this QR code to see examples of digital Canva OneNote templates that you can customize!

Scan this QR code to see additional Canva lessons.

Coaches' Corner

Canva is a teacher's creation zone! You can create coordinated classroom *everything*—themed planners, presentations, worksheets, physical labels for your classroom, Teams announcement headers (the Google header templates work), class rules, lesson plan templates, and more! Sign up for your *free* educator account and start exploring!

PART FOUR

Practice Makes Perfect

CHAPTER 12

Fine-Tune Your Coaching Skills

Throughout this manual, we have served as your coaches. You have identified how to leverage technology to equal the playing field for your students, you have learned best practices for using Teams in your classroom, and you have access to a playbook of Teams and partner application plays to use. Now it's time to play!

As you continue to play in the role of teacher, of course, you also serve as a coach to your students and, perhaps, other teachers. As such, we encourage you to continue to grow your coaching skills. As we wrap up this book, we will share some tools we recommend.

MIE (Microsoft Innovator Educator) Family

We are extremely thankful for the relationships we have gained from being part of the Microsoft Innovator Educator family. Our Microsoft community truly is family to us. In fact, this book wouldn't have been possible without them. We have benefited greatly from being MIE Experts, and we strongly recommend your becoming part of this group.

Scan this QR code to learn more about joining this awesome community of educators.

Microsoft Educator Center

In Part Three of this book, we have shared numerous MEC (Microsoft Educator Center) lessons in our Scouting Profiles as well as resources or courses supporting the lessons. MEC is a one-stop shop for all your K–12 teaching and learning needs. It is also a great resource for those in higher education. This platform is constantly growing and improving.

Some of our favorite ways to use the MEC include the following:

- Earn badges and certificates.
- Become an MIE Expert through earning points and completing the self-nomination process each spring.
- Connect with and learn from educators across the globe.
- Participate in global projects.
- View webinars and online events.
- Learn all you need to know about Minecraft and Hacking STEM.
- Share resources for parents.

If you are not already a member of the Microsoft Educator Center, scan this QR code to get started.

Scan this QR code to view the various MEC courses related to tools we identified throughout the book. You may have seen these on the Scouting Profile for each application/tool, but this link will take you directly to the Wakelet MEC Training/Resources Space.

Social Media

Jenallee believes in and encourages lifelong learning. Personally, we love learning something new, blogging about it, tweeting about it, or making a YouTube video highlighting our new learning. We may even make a TikTok about it (actually, *Salleé* will make the TikTok! She has mastered her TikTok skills!)

Our favorite way to learn is by connecting with others, often through social media. We have built relationships with many other lifelong learners and then shared learning with them. In turn, we love sharing with others on social media the new tips and tricks we learn.

Scan this QR code to get connected to other educators and edtech companies! Subscribe to YouTube channels, follow Instagram and Twitter accounts, become friends on Facebook, and follow the incredible TikToks accounts noted.

Ambassador Programs

Many of the applications and tools we have shared with you have "ambassador programs" or offer a community you can engage with and become part of. As we have noted, we think it is imperative you find a PLN to connect and share with and learn from. The programs noted below may become your PLN or, through them, you will likely meet individuals to include in your PLN.

These communities offer many advantages—webinars, Twitter chats, swag, speaking engagements, upgraded accounts, Twitter DM groups, Facebook interactions, and much more.

Below is a brief list of the opportunities available through the companies or tools we have highlighted in this book.

Company/Tool	Ambassador/Community Program	Benefits/Opportunities
Microsoft EDU	MIE Expert family	Monthly calls Monthly newsletter Travel program options Twitter connections Webinars Facebook community Badges
Genially	Ambassador program	Upgraded account Webinars
Flipgrid	Community member, Ambassador program, and Certified Educator	Badges Webinars Facebook community
Buncee	Ambassador program	Monthly calls Upgraded account Facebook community Badges
Adobe	Founding crew and Creative Educator levels	Upgraded accounts Webinars Creative challenges/levels Facebook community
Wakelet	Community member and Ambassadors for teachers and students	Webinars Twitter DM group Badges
Canva	Educator account for *free*	Facebook community Webinars
Whiteboard.chat	Ambassador	Webinars 1:1 Zoom meetings Facebook community

Bibliography

Clark, H. (2020). *The Chromebook Infused Classroom: Using Blended Learning to Create Engaging Student Centered Classrooms*. Elevate Books Edu.

Clark, H., and Avrith, T. (2020). *The Microsoft Infused Classroom*. Elevate Books Edu.

"Grant Wiggins: Defining Assessment." *Edutopia*. (2021). Retrieved July 2, 2021, from https://www.edutopia.org/grant-wiggins-assessment.

Hattie, J. (2012). *Visible Learning for Teachers: Maximizing Impact on Learning*. Routledge.

Highfill, L., Hilton, K., and Landis, S. (2019). *The HyperDoc Handbook: Digital Lesson Design Using Google Apps*. Elevate Books Edu.

"How Can Teachers Nurture Meaningful Student Agency? MindShift." *KQED*. (2021). Retrieved July 2, 2021, from https://www.kqed.org/mindshift/56946/how-can-teachers-nurture-meaningful-student-agency?fbclid=IwAR0uGs10jg8kPor7P7d9UXiFQXOWhZv9FaUOGqRur-29BgjBOUX2JdwgzMRo.

MacKenzie, T., and Bathurst, R. (2019). *The Inquiry Mindset*. Elevate Books Edu.

"Manage the Whiteboard in Microsoft Teams." (2021). Retrieved July 3, 2021, from https://docs.microsoft.com/en-us/microsoftteams/manage-whiteboard.

Microsoft Teams. Support.microsoft.com. (2021). Retrieved July 2, 2021, from https://support.microsoft.com/en-us/topic/microsoft-teams-5aa4431a-8a3c-4aa5-87a6-b6401abea114?ui=en-us&rs=en-us&ad=us.

"Microsoft Teams Education: How to Manage It Like a Pro." *Ditch That Textbook*. (2021). Retrieved July 3, 2021, from https://ditchthattextbook.com/microsoft-teams.

Rath, T. (2007). *Strengths Finder 2.0*. Gallup Press.

"Updates—Flipgrid." *Flipgrid*. (2021). Retrieved July 2, 2021, from https://blog.flipgrid.com/updates.

"What is Genius Hour?" *Genius Hour*. (2021). Retrieved July 2, 2021, from http://geniushour.com/what-is-genius-hour.

Wiggins, G., and McTighe, J. (2005). *Understanding by Design*. Association for Supervision & Curriculum Development.

Wong, H. (1998). *The First Days of School*. Harry K. Wong Publications.

About the Authors

Jeni Long

Jeni Long is a wife and a very active mother of four, three girls and one boy. Jeni and her family live in Ft. Worth, Texas, where they enjoy traveling, supporting each other in school activities, lounging by the pool, family movie nights, and playing with their two labradoodles, Toby and Luke. In her spare time, Jeni enjoys running, riding her Peloton, laying by the pool, going to church, and spending time with friends and family. Jeni loves creating and sharing educational content with her best friend and coworker, Salleé. Together they love to present, create, laugh, and connect with educators across the globe. Jeni loves presenting at conferences and reuniting with friends and teachers everywhere.

Salleé Clark

Salleé Clark is a wife and mother who loves to spend time traveling, playing games, sharing the love of Jesus, and hanging out with family and friends. Her travels have taught her the value of different viewpoints and ideas. Through educational technology, Salleé has bridged her love of people and education. Technology affords her the ability to learn with a global family of educators that are seeking to empower their scholars to do more than ever before! Salleé loves her job and working with her best friend, Jeni. They work on an amazing team who passionately serves teachers and students every day!

Invite Jenallee to Speak at Your Next Professional Development Event

Jeni and Salleé are international speakers, edtech consultants, bloggers, and authors. They currently serve as Instructional Technologists with Eagle Mountain-Saginaw ISD in Fort Worth, Texas. This dynamic duo, known as "Jenallee," is passionate about technology integration and making learning accessible, equitable, and fun for all!

Jeni and Salleé cohost a YouTube show called *The Jenallee Show*. Their blog and YouTube show highlight the newest edtech tools and offer tech tutorials for educators across the globe.

Both Jeni and Salleé have earned Masters of Educational Technology degrees and together they have more than thirty-seven years' experience in education. They have presented sessions at BETT, TCEA, FETC, ISTE, and various other conferences as featured and keynote speakers. They are both MIE Experts and Minecraft Trainers, as well as ambassadors for Wakelet, Buncee, Genially, Adobe, Whiteboard.chat, Beedle, and Flipgrid. In addition, both Jeni and Salleé have served their MIE community as MIE Fellows.

Jenallee recently won the Social Media Master award from the MIE Expert community. They have also written articles for *Tech and Learning* and are collaborating authors on the book *Amplify Learning: A Global Collaborative,* which will be released in early 2022.

Within the Microsoft community, Jenallee enjoys presenting on webinars, creating content for the MEC, and consulting for a team of amazing educators with the Microsoft Training Partner, Ed to the Max. In addition to consulting with Microsoft, Jenallee serves the global education community through Jenallee, LLC.

Jenallee seeks to learn, share, and empower their community with edtech tools. Connecting and collaborating with educators from around the world has made Jenallee better educators, people, and trainers.

Jenallee would love to work with you! Scan this QR code to learn more about Jenallee and their work within the educational technology community.

About the Illustrator

Julie Woodard

Julie Woodard is an educator who has enjoyed teaching in Texas public education for the past twenty years. She is also an edudoodler, sketch-noter, and edugraphic artist who has connected with authors, speakers, presenters, and educators around the world.

She creates images to illustrate ideas and information in ways that lift, support, and encourage educators to work collectively to empower and inspire students toward greatness. "If we go beyond connecting to collaborating, I believe we can reach our students in truly amazing and meaningful ways," she says.

Connect with Julie Woodward

S'more link: smore.com/fmdva-woodstock-images

Twitter: @woodard_julie

Made in the USA
Coppell, TX
25 October 2021